"*Logically Accurate, Emotionally Healthy* represents an evolutionary upgrade in the way we understand and apply thinking to our everyday lives. Dr Sean Eastwood has created a template which, if practically applied, will revolutionise the way we approach mind-body health care now and in the future."

Dr Peter Grant
Chiropractor/NET Practitioner

"What a mind job! Dr Sean's book *Logically Accurate, Emotionally Healthy* brings more depth, reality and detail to our non-physical mind. Dr Sean shares a framework of mind processing to train your mind and its thought process to be more *Logically Accurate, Emotionally Healthy.*"

Dr George Gonzalez, DC
Founder of Quantum Neurology
Nervous System Rehabilitation
www.QuantumNeurology.com

"With depression, addiction, PTSD and beyond becoming a mental health crisis, Dr Sean's book *Logically Accurate, Emotionally Healthy* explains the complex nature of the mind with a natural law of thought. Whether you are totally focused on performance excellence or have just a passing interest in the emotional health of you and your family – this book is for you. A step by step, easy to follow, structured system. I believe it should be taught in schools. I have never seen anything like it before."

Michael Blake
Former NRL Player

"It is said that your thoughts create your reality, but the creative process by which this happens is not well understood. Indeed, the human brain is the most complex biological structure ever to have existed on this planet. Having it is like putting an average driver behind the wheel of the most powerful sports car. Without knowledge and skill, it is easy to lose control. I recommend Dr Sean Eastwood's breakthrough book *Logically Accurate, Emotionally Healthy* as a readable user guide for anyone wanting to improve their quality of life."

David Tuffley, PhD

"Dr Sean provides step by step blueprints for human thought and perception that fit seamlessly with the mindfulness and energy psychology techniques that I've learned. *Logically Accurate, Emotionally Healthy* is the first self-development book everyone should read because it's true – everything begins with a thought!"

Peter Ristovski
Retail Specialist

"A text that is challenging to the absolute core of our understanding – dense with knowledge and penetrative insights."

Dr Andrew Macfarlane
Chiropractor

"*Logically Accurate, Emotionally Healthy* has profound ramifications for anyone seriously trying to understand the power of their mind to create their own happiness and free themselves from the self-doubt of unhealthy, unstructured thinking. Dr Sean has reinforced my belief in the inherent goodness of the human spirit."

Asha Sanders
Missionary, Myanmar

"I can now think through day to day situations without them becoming a threat to my daily harmony. Dr Eastwood breaks down a large volume of knowledge into building blocks that help to logically disarm the power of the emotional charge."

Jennifer Morgan
Stage Production

"I recommend Dr Sean Eastwood's book *Logically Accurate, Emotionally Healthy* and consider it a breakthrough in understanding the human thought process. The subject is well explained and systematically it builds up to a mind-blowing experience of the human thought process."

Marianne Winter
Transformational Life Coach/Trainer

"We are all in this game of life together and if we are all on the same page there would be no conflicts between one another or wars among nations. This book by Dr Sean Eastwood is the recipe for that one page to lead us to live in harmony, as one."

Rod McCagh
Retired Farmer

Logically Accurate, Emotionally Healthy

Dr Sean Eastwood

First published 2021 by Dr Sean Eastwood

Produced by Indie Experts P/L, Australasia
indieexperts.com.au

Copyright © Dr Sean Eastwood 2021

The moral right of the author to be identified as the author of this work has been asserted.

Except for the purposes of reviewing, no part of this publication may be reproduced or transmitted in any form or by any means, electronic or mechanical, including photocopying, recording or any information storage or retrieval system, without the written permission of the author. Infringers of copyright render themselves liable for prosecution.

Cover design by Daniela Catucci @ Catucci Design
Edited by Anne-Marie Tripp @ Indie Experts
Internal design by Indie Experts
Typeset in 10/16 pt Europa by Post Pre-press Group, Brisbane

ISBN 978-0-6452395-0-8 (paperback)
ISBN 978-0-6452395-1-5 (epub)

Disclaimer: The information and opinions expressed in this publication belong to the author, and do not reflect the views or opinions held by the publishers or their respective employees and agents. The information contained in this book is for educational purposes only, and does not substitute professional medical advice. Please consult with your healthcare provider for individually tailored advice, diagnoses, or treatment. Every effort has been made to ensure this publication is as accurate and complete as possible; however, the author and the publisher assume no responsibility for any errors, inaccuracies, omissions, or other inconsistencies contained herein. The author, publisher, and their respective employees and agents shall not be liable or responsible to any person or entity for any loss or damage caused or alleged to have been caused directly or indirectly by the information contained in this book.

This book is dedicated to medical general practitioners – GPs who are the first responders to the global mental health crisis and who dedicate their working lives to helping others, at a potential risk to their own mental and physical wellbeing and with minimal public recognition.

As primary healthcare providers, mental health is only one of a seemingly endless list of conditions that GPs must contend with. Without forewarning, any given patient visit can range from a head cold to an undiagnosed terminal illness. At the other end of the emotional spectrum, GPs share the joy of new-borns coming into the world, the satisfaction of knowing that they have saved someone's life and the heart-felt appreciation from patients for the care received.

Stress isn't always constant – it can be unexpected, intermittent and vary in type and intensity. Society can learn a great deal about stress management from highly intelligent, compassionate people who have to maintain emotional balance in a taxing work environment – and then extend that emotional balance to their personal lives.

When a solution to the global mental health crisis is found, it certainly won't involve a lack of well-trained, compassionate healthcare professionals – it therefore must involve a societal shift created by a scientific breakthrough.

Contents

Foreword 1

Part 1: Setting the Stage — 5

"The Ox is Slow but the Earth is Patient."
- 1: Dr Sean's Story — 7
- 2: Where a Winding Road Can Lead You — 9
- 3: Awestruck by a Spreadsheet — 11
- 4: Solving Problems in My Sleep — 13
- 5: My Introduction to Artificial General Intelligence (AGI) — 17
- 6: A Unifying Theory of Human Health and Computer Science — 20

Part 2: The Curtain Rises — 23

The Characters and Their Makeup
- 7: The Old Paradigm — 25
- 8: Simplify and Rationalise — 28
- 9: Function and Structure — 31
- 10: Emotional Patterns — 35
- 11: Including All the Variables — 37
- 12: What the Hell Is a Fractal? — 42
- 13: Life Lessons – Correcting Fractal Patterns — 44
- 14: Our Progress So Far! — 47
- 15: Where Do Beliefs Come From? — 49
- 16: Types of Beliefs — 54
- 17: Shock and Awe — 60
- 18: Tolerance Range of a Belief — 65

Part 3: A Recurring Theme — 69

The Quest for a Competent Mind
- 19: Competency Model of Learning — 71
- 20: Competency Model of Thinking — 75
- 21: Integrative Competence — 78
- 22: Collective Competence — 82
- 23: A Competent Mind — 84

Part 4: The Love Story   87

Perception Completes Thought While Logic and Emotion Wave

   24: Modelling the New Information   89
   25: Fractal Plasticity   92
   26: An Advanced Philosophical Model of Health   94
   27: Thought Creates Perception   96
   28: Fractal Mindset Blueprint   98
   29: The Thought Process Is a Talent Contest   106

Part 5: Unexpected Twists and Turns   111

The Genius of Fractal Design

   30: Fractal Symmetry   113
   31: Fractal Pairing   116
   32: Executing the Preparation of the Decision   118
   33: Preparing for the Execution of the Decision   121
   34: Fractal Pairing and Pattern Recognition   123
   35: Fractal Branching   126
   36: Fractal Trilogy   129
   37: Fractal Reduction   132

Part 6: The Encore and a Hint of Sequels!   135

Fractal Design – The Shape of Things to Come

   38: The Future of All Training   137
   39: Standardised Communication   140
   40: Training in Collective Consciousness   142
   41: Fractal Pairing and DNA   144

Part 7: The Star Revealed   147

The Curtain Falls

   42: The Logic of the Master Algorithm   149
   43: An Australian Software Developer   151

Acknowledgements   155
Thought Martial Arts Online Courses   157
About the Author   159

Foreword

The greatest discovery in human history will be the sequential recipe for optimal human thought. It will foreshadow a solution to the global mental health crisis and provide the logic of the master algorithm of "true" artificial intelligence.

Does this book contain the holy grail of both human health and computer science? I believe so – but the truth only has one friend and that's time!

My guarantee is that you will never have seen a more complete explanation of human thought and perception that can be applied to the time machine of your mind and your every thought of the past, present and future.

This book provides the underlying rules or code to every personal development program that you will ever attend and every self-help book that you will ever read.

It delivers street maps for stress-reduction, mindfulness and healing techniques which are the street sweepers of emotional debris.

It provides a mechanism to standardise your personal and inter-personal communication and empowers you to calibrate your thinking to the thought processes of others.

Possibly most importantly, it highlights the building blocks of perception that will enable future generations to think in emotional patterns. Identifying an emotionally healthy pattern in the same way that an experienced card player identifies a winning hand.

Logically Accurate, Emotionally Healthy is based on two fundamental principles.

1. The human thought process is a natural law like gravity.

2. Everything in your existence begins with a thought.

We are not taught how to think optimally. Therefore, we have a social crisis of unhealthy, unstructured thinking that jackpots into a global mental health crisis. Simultaneously, we can't program computers to mimic optimal human thought to create "true" artificial intelligence.

Since 2013, I have been studying the work of a now-deceased Australian software engineer who claimed to have discovered the master algorithm of "true" artificial intelligence based on a discovery he made in 1999, that the human thought process is a natural law like gravity.

My contribution, based on this gentleman's work, are blueprints for human thought and perception that have the branching, tree-like design that is inherent in all nature. Fractal algorithms that are as easy to learn as playing hopscotch.

I investigated the possibility of enrolling in a PhD with the subject of this book being my thesis. The advice I received was that science is built on pre-existing science. It appears there is no scientific precedent for the presentation of a natural law for the human thought process which creates a natural law for human perception and models variables which accommodate all forms of physical and energetic medicine. I was advised to write a book as they are more widely read than scientific papers in any event.

This book is written for the unborn generations of your family. Please read this information through their eyes. It foreshadows a solution to the global mental health crisis based on prevention and scientific education, particularly of our children.

The Universe is based on cause, effect and natural laws. The time has come for self-aware and well-intentioned people around the world to stand as one to address the social crisis of unhealthy, unstructured thinking that jackpots into the global medical crisis in mental health – at a seemingly ever-increasing rate.

The practical application of this knowledge and how it can be combined with stress-reduction, mindfulness and healing techniques is the subject of the Thought Martial Arts online courses. How to ask questions of your mindset to identify unhealthy beliefs and enhance emotional health is a skillset that we should be taught from childhood.

I have seen the waste involved when someone takes to their grave revolutionary information that could have profoundly benefited humanity. Publishing this book provides a great sense of relief in not making the same mistake.

I hope this information enriches your life as much as it continues to enrich mine.

Part 1
Setting the Stage

"The Ox is Slow but the
Earth is Patient."
— Tibetan Proverb

1: Dr Sean's Story

One of my earliest memories, real or imagined, from around 2 years of age, is standing alone in my parent's kitchen and hearing on the radio that something called the "Cuban Missile Crisis", involving a "nuclear war", threatened to kill every human on the planet because world leaders were unhappy with each other.

I have no recollection of being scared by this news. My only memory was being thoroughly disgusted at how so-called "clever" people could be so stupid as to think that killing everyone on the planet was in anyone's best interests.

On reflection, not understanding things was a deeply ingrained default response for me whilst growing up. I couldn't understand why people couldn't just get on with their life and leave others to their business. I couldn't understand why there were so many rules around the home and at school. I couldn't understand why these rules were inconsistently enforced.

Having a religious Mother, I couldn't understand how a loving God could send you to hell for breaching rules that you didn't even know existed. I couldn't understand how you could be guilty of the "sin of pride" if you didn't have any sins to admit to the priest at your weekly confession … the list went on.

Fundamentally though, I'd formed the belief that if I was a good person, then good things should happen. Very early in life, I'm sure that I made that contract with the Universe! Anything that didn't subsequently meet with my Universe-ordained personal approval represented a breach of contract for which the Universe owed me an explanation, apology and some form of compensation.

In reality, all that had happened was that I'd told myself a whole lot of logically inaccurate and emotionally unhealthy stories – and ran with them. In other words, I had never been trained how to think effectively and optimally, reflecting and correcting where needed to create and automate logically accurate and emotionally healthy beliefs.

In the years that I've spent studying "intelligence", one of the biggest "aha!" game-changing moments has been the realisation that emotional stress invariably results from the fact that you are an inherently good person who has never recovered from the shock of a noble, healthy belief being compromised.

You deserve to feel safe, loved and nurtured to your potential; but it's the stories that you tell yourself when these noble healthy beliefs are compromised that determines your emotional health.

But, more on this later!

2: Where a Winding Road Can Lead You

There's something humiliating about telling team mates that you can't play rugby league for 4 weeks because you put your back out washing your feet in the shower; particularly when they had seen you pack into 20 scrums a couple of days before with no ill effect to your physical demeanour or your post-match thirst.

At the time, I'd moved to Toowoomba in Queensland, Australia from the Gold Coast to study accountancy at the Darling Downs Institute of Advanced Education, which later became the University of Southern Queensland.

The move was inspired by a notice of academic exclusion that I'd received for failing 7 out of 10 subjects over a 2-year period while studying as a distance education student. The compromise to let me continue my studies was for me to become a fulltime, on-campus student.

In my defence, I was straight out of school, working fulltime and living in the party capital of Australia – but even at school, study wasn't my thing and I was always in the "dumb class".

What accountancy did teach me, however, is the need for balance in a complex system. Irrespective of how many millions of dollars you are dealing with, if the books don't balance, there is a mistake and you must backtrack to find what has gone wrong and where.

The balance that the human body craves — and will sabotage itself to maintain — is called homeostasis. As we'll discuss, the dysfunction of ill health occurs when there is a distortion in the inherent design of the body. Restoring balance is the key to resolving ill health.

Unknowingly, the experience of recurring and chronic back problems sparked my fascination with mind/body medicine. Over a long period, I was seeing good GPs, chiropractors and physiotherapists but none could answer the question of why I was seemingly fit, yet had a back that could just "give" on me.

3: Awestruck by a Spreadsheet

The back problem was still an issue in my late 20s, by which time I'd spent 3 years in Papua New Guinea installing mainframe accounting systems. Personal computers were becoming popular and I'd been exposed to an amazing piece of software called a "spreadsheet".

The interconnectedness created by information being stored in the rows and columns of a table, with any given cell of the spreadsheet able to change the value of potentially all the other cells, was amazing to me. An ability to think in tables served me well during my anatomy studies in remembering the interconnectedness between nerves, muscles, joints, organs, patterns of sensation of the skin, etc.

Understanding spreadsheets has also helped me understand how the human thought process can be expressed as a mathematical formula with each of the variables in the equation having values which can be updated. Updating the value of an unhealthy emotion, for example, can change the value of a belief from unhealthy to healthy.

Imagine every cell in your body equating to every cell in a spreadsheet. In terms of your health, the aim is for every cell to have a healthy value. Any cell in your body has the potential to affect the cells around it and your entire body is a fully-integrated system of systems.

4: Solving Problems in My Sleep

If a bad back was the spark for my interest in human health, then the experience of solving computer-programming problems in my sleep was well and truly the fuel that inspired me to start reading books on the subconscious.

By that stage, I'd returned to Toowoomba after stints in Northern Ireland and England and was working for the Toowoomba City Council as one of their accounting managers. In the early 1990s Australia was reviewing its infrastructure for the provision of water services. To decrease demand, it was changing to a user pays model of pricing per kilolitre rather than an allowance-based system where you paid for a sizable allowance of water irrespective of how much you consumed, and were only charged per kilolitre if you exceeded the allowance.

I was assigned the task of developing a spreadsheet-based model to measure the effect that any given pricing change would have on revenue – which I did. Realising the potential of business consultancy in this field, I resigned from the Toowoomba City Council but then had to reverse engineer the spreadsheet model formulas that I had developed as an employee to ensure that there was no breach of intellectual property laws.

Redesigning the formulas of the model hit a snag and I spent 10 hours a day for about a week on one line of code trying to trick the spreadsheet software to do something that, in the earliest versions, it wasn't designed to do. To make matters worse, subconsciously I was mentally rehearsing this line of code all night in my sleep and waking up exhausted.

Eventually I went to bed one night and in an attempt to get some peaceful sleep, said to myself, "For God's sake! Stop trying to solve the problem by going over every permutation and combination of that line of code in your head!" Turns out I did. I woke up at 3:00 a.m. simply knowing what the line of code was without any mental rehearsing. Even before I typed that code into the computer and pressed enter, I knew it would work.

On reflection, if I'd have simply said, "Stop trying to solve the problem in your sleep!", my subconscious would have switched off and a solution would have evaded me. I believe that "intelligence" exists and can be tapped into but you have to be very precise in what you ask for.

So, I started reading books on the subconscious hoping to learn techniques to "sleep-solve" problems, but the focus of all these books was on healing. Despite having a bad back, poor digestion and prone to being cantankerous, I failed to see any personal relevance.

Mind/Body Medicine

By now it was the mid 1990s and I was playing cricket in Toowoomba with a chiropractor named Dr Andrew Macfarlane who was learning a lot of the latest neurological work coming out of America at the time. Dr Andrew also had an aeroplane pilot's licence and worked clinics in country towns around South West Queensland. He had free lodgings at my place, so long as I received a complimentary chiropractic adjustment whenever he stayed over.

Dr Andrew started treating my back complaint to great effect with a stress-reduction technique that identified a weakness in my spine attributed to a stressful experience from childhood. I still remember the shock of realising the extent to which our thoughts, emotions and health are inextricably intertwined. I also became acutely aware that I was responsible for my every thought of the past, present and future – not a very appealing proposition at the time.

I was fortunate enough to be the patient of a very well-respected GP in the district named Dr Dilip Dhupelia. When told of the improvement in my back from a mind/body technique, he gave me advice that I have given patients for 20 years – "go where you get results!"

These experiences were the catalysts for a journey that has seen me change professions; return to university for 5 years in my late 30s to retrain as a chiropractor; travel to the USA repeatedly to be mentored by a leading authority in mind/body medicine and attend many seminars in Australia from outstanding teachers and mentors in the field of complementary and alternative medicine.

These teachers and mentors include Drs Scott and Deb Walker, co-developers of Neuro Emotional Technique; Dr Alan Phillips, founder of Neurological Integration System; Dr George Gonzalez, founder of Quantum Neurology; Dr Igor Tabrizian, founder of Health Quest; and more recently Dr Joe Dispenza, chiropractor, neurologist and bestselling author.

In terms of opportunity cost, repayment of loans to finance my studies, seminar fees, travel, accommodation and donations to research organisations, I have lost track of the financial commitment. Despite being a qualified accountant, money has never really motivated me. On my deathbed, the thought of my net worth will run a far distant second to an audit of my own heart and my intentions to other people ... that's the plan anyway.

5: My Introduction to Artificial General Intelligence (AGI)

I apologise in advance for the "nerd factor" of the next few paragraphs. For ease of understanding, the information is visually mapped out in diagrams in later chapters.

This information is designed to help you understand the journey of discovery that I've been on to present this work. More importantly it helps you understand the overlap between human health and computer science. Future generations will see this overlap as self-evident and blatantly obvious. In my case, it took me about 2 years of focus to really get my head around the topic.

Artificial general intelligence (AGI) for the purposes of this book is defined as "a computer program that mimics optimal human thought". Computers are programmed using algorithms; an algorithm being a sequential series of executable steps that produces a perfect result in a minimum number of steps.

The definitive, or master algorithm for AGI therefore must be a sequential series of executable steps that creates optimal human thought.

There are two broad schools of thinking about the discovery of AGI. One is that it will be discovered by self-improving computer programs that will eventually "learn" their way to the optimal algorithm for the human thought process. The other is that the human thought process is a yet-to-be-discovered natural law like gravity. The same way that Einstein's famous formula $E=mc^2$ always existed, but until its discovery was unknown.

As I'll demonstrate, I'm in no doubt that the human thought process is not only a natural law, but the perception that is created by the thought process is also a natural law. Going one step further, both of these natural laws have the inherent design of nature which is a fractal – a simple recurring process with an ever-present, self-correction mechanism. The self-correction mechanism is your power of free will to reflect and correct unhealthy beliefs.

My view is that a fractal algorithm for the human thought process is a major milestone on the path to Singularity – a term computer experts use to explain the explosion of innovation and discovery that will occur as machine learning approximates human intelligence. What I refer to as the Fractal Mindset Blueprint and the Fractal Perception Blueprint are evidence of this innovation and discovery.

Show Me the Money!

The most lucrative application of AGI is to provide the advanced encryption, computing power and search engine capability required to create what is generally referred to as the Internet of Things and then clip the ticket, via a processing fee, on every transaction of global e-commerce. This was my inspiration for investing in artificial intelligence, beginning in 2008.

It wasn't until 2013 that I realised that the founder of the company that I had invested in was saying that human thought was a natural law and that he had discovered the logic of it in 1999. He shared the logic of this natural law with me, and I made certain translations and observations relating to human health.

Unbeknown to him, I spent the next 6 months proving to my own satisfaction only one step in his model. That is, if you have an unhealthy emotional reflex to a life event, then you have either lost faith in a healthy belief, invested faith in an unhealthy belief, or both. Proving this one step meant that the other steps fell into place like falling dominoes.

6: A Unifying Theory of Human Health and Computer Science

A mathematical model for the human thought process means that practitioners, or individuals working by themselves, not only have a pro forma guide for healthy, structured thinking, they also have a blueprint to track up and back through the thought processes of emotionally damaging experiences to help address the negative effects on mind, body and spirit, using the stress-reduction, mindfulness and healing techniques of their choice.

Stress-reduction, mindfulness and healing techniques are the street sweepers of emotional debris. A mathematical model for the human thought process provides a street map to guide the way.

Before Pasteur and other scientists, we were unconsciously incompetent about the knowledge that germs cause infection. The global mental health crisis means that we must be overlooking a basic law of science and nature.

The Fractal Mindset Blueprint is a unifying theory of human health and computer science – a formula for human thought with the inherent design of nature. It is a sequential series of steps with an ever-present, self-correction mechanism that produces a perfect result in a minimum number of steps – a fractal algorithm.

The cornerstone of the science of chemistry is the periodic table – a list of elements in ascending order of their atomic number which provides structure and insight into the interconnected workings of nature. The science of your mind now has the Fractal Mindset Blueprint – a mathematical formula for the thought process that creates human perception.

Alan Turing, famous for shortening World War II by cracking German ciphers (as depicted in the movie *The Imitation Game*), merged mathematics, computer science, psychology and philosophy to create machine learning. The Fractal Blueprint Series is an extension of Turing's work as it applies to human health.

The only way to understand your mindset is to understand the thought process that creates it. You are already closer to achieving this than you may think because you are already aware of the pieces of the puzzle. It is the purpose of the puzzle and the internal dynamic that holds the puzzle together that needs fine tuning.

Part 2
The Curtain Rises

The Characters and Their Makeup

7: The Old Paradigm

A paradigm is simply a set of rules by which you understand a given topic. When faced with a new paradigm, an understanding of how the new rules are an improvement on the old rules is required.

For example, as a kid I loved mangoes. As a treat, I'd get thrown in an empty bathtub with my speedos on and given a peeled whole mango to eat. I'd then get hosed down to continue my day. In my 20s, I learned the paradigm shift of cutting the cheeks off a mango, dicing the flesh, then inverting the cheek to be presented with readily accessible mango cubes. Eating a mango, without having to simultaneously wear it, is a life hack that I'll enjoy 'til my grave.

To investigate the potential paradigm shift that human health and computer science were related by a mathematical formula for human thought, I re-examined the mind/body techniques that I had studied to try and understand a common rationale behind them. My original thinking was that there had to be a separate natural law of emotions if there was a natural law of thought.

Most mind/body techniques teach that, based on your existing beliefs, a life event creates an emotion which in turn creates a new belief or re-enforces an existing belief – healthy or unhealthy. I refer to this model as the Old School Model of Emotions & Beliefs.

Old School Model of Emotions & Beliefs

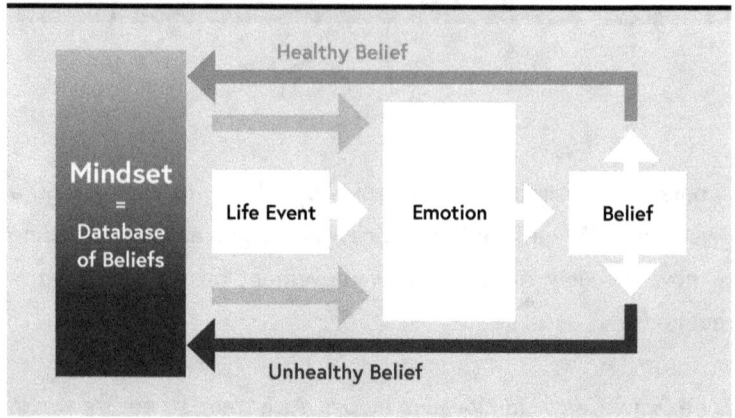

By way of example, let's take a childhood life event of being bitten by a big, brown, male dog – for dramatic effect, let's call him "Killer". This experience may inspire many different emotions but let's focus on the single emotion of fear, which will create a belief that Killer is dangerous.

If that belief becomes reflexive, then all subsequent life events of being exposed to Killer will inspire the emotion of fear. If that belief and emotional reflex is then subconsciously generalised, exaggerated and catastrophised, any future life event with any dog – irrespective of size, colour or gender – will inspire fear.

This reflexive fear of dogs may then extend to "Bambi", the white, female, miniature Chihuahua and runt of its litter. Whilst a proportionate fear of dogs, including Killer, is healthy, a disproportionate fear is not.

The question must then be asked: "Is the Old School Model sufficiently detailed to accommodate all the variables of the Killer/Bambi experience?"

The answer is a resounding NO!

8: Simplify and Rationalise

When you are trying to create a visual model of something intricate, a trick that I learned as a computer systems analyst is to differentiate between the variables of a problem and all the values that a variable may have – and only include variables.

In the Old School Model, whether a belief is historic or the subject of the current thought process it's the same variable of belief. The same rule applies to the values of healthy or unhealthy beliefs. Using one variable for belief greatly simplifies our fledgling model of perception and highlights necessary enhancements.

Rationalised Old School Model

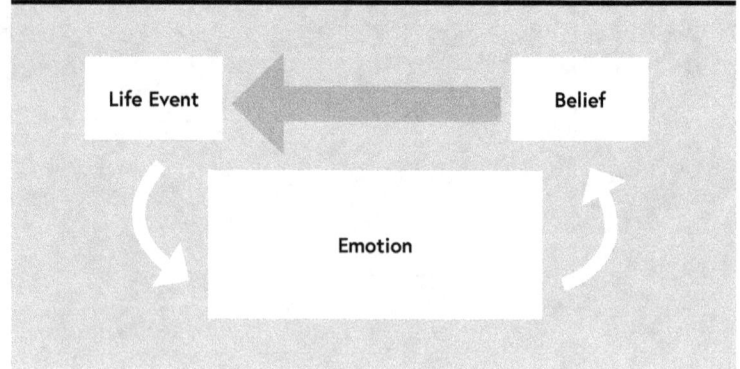

Apart from looking much less cluttered, the first encouraging observation is that we are obviously dealing with a very simple recurring process – which is exactly what thinking involves. The second is that there is a symmetry to the model which is a fundamental characteristic of nature – something that we elaborate on later.

There are three major weaknesses in the Rationalised Old School Model. These will be the focus of the next few chapters.

1. The perception of a belief involves far more than just the assignment of an emotion. Identifying these other variables and their significance is imperative to the integrity of a model for perception.

2. Intelligence is about self-correction. There is no mechanism in the Old School Model to exercise your power of free will to reflect and correct an unhealthy belief.

3. There is no triggering mechanism illustrated to explain what inspires an unhealthy emotion to a life event. What is the characteristic of a belief that triggers an unhealthy emotional response to a life event?

The Rationalised Old School Model is about to undergo a process of metamorphosis; firstly, into a comprehensive model for human perception which I call the Fractal Perception Blueprint, and then into what I believe to be a sequential series of steps and mathematical model for optimal human thought – the Fractal Mindset Blueprint.

Fractal Perception Blueprint

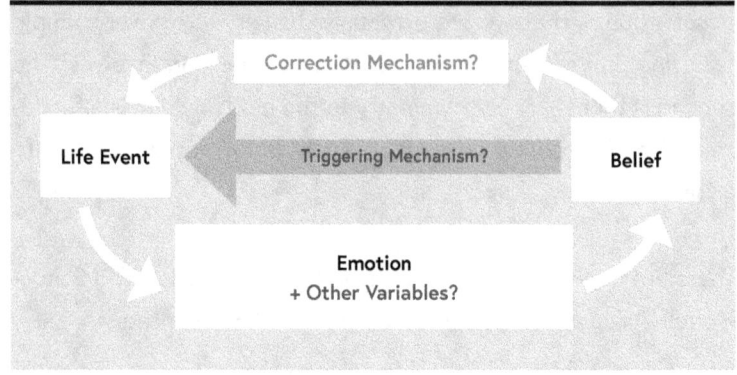

Also, because perception is created by a thought process, a longer model for the thought process must truncate to a shorter model of perception. This relationship between thought and perception needs to be clearly visible in their respective mathematical models.

So, get comfortable. Our journey of discovery will be taken in a sequential, easy to follow format with plenty of real-life examples. You can't explain the purpose and structure of the human condition without touching on some deep content at times. If there is any topic that you can't readily grasp, my advice is to skim forward and come back to it later. The subconscious mind understands and later reveals far more than we give it credit for.

Having failed my first semester of mathematics in year 11 at school I can assure you that sometimes the difference between not knowing and knowing something can take just seconds.

From studying this work, I am convinced that Galileo was correct when he said that "Mathematics is the language in which God wrote the Universe!"

9: Function and Structure

What Does It Do? What Does It Look Like?

With the mental health crisis unfolding over the last couple of decades, there have been reports that anxiety and depression are expected to be the norm in future generations. With such compassionate, well trained people working in the mental health industry and the supporting infrastructures of government, charities, community, business and employee networks and the education system, this current and continuing disaster makes absolutely no sense to me.

Two questions are fundamental to any scientific inquiry – what does it do and what does it look like? So, if we are to prevent the unnecessary suffering of future generations, we must ask the following questions:

1. If we have 50,000 plus thoughts a day, what is the purpose of human thought? What does it do?

2. If the fabric of our life is based on recurring emotional patterns, what are the building blocks of a pattern? What does an emotional pattern look like?

I believe the solution to both questions lies in understanding illustrative models for the human thought process, ones that can be taught to our kids from early childhood. So, let's get a handle on what a mathematical model actually is.

Variables, Values and Patterns

There are many benefits to having a mathematical model to solve problems. By knowing all the variables of a scenario and assigning them values, you can identify patterns to remember the past and predict the future. Pattern formation and pattern recognition are fundamental characteristics of intelligence.

For example, a junior athlete can be profiled for senior success on the performance "variables" of size, speed and strength. Performance "values" of junior athletes can be assessed against known successful senior athletes to establish the "pattern" of a future star athlete.

In a different application, businesses can have an exhaustive list of key performance indicators (KPIs) for profit margins, revenue growth, customer retention, staff turnover, inventory levels, debt ratios – the list goes on. KPIs are used as building blocks to assess the pattern for a successful, profitable business.

In attempting to understand intelligence, computer scientists have done a lot of work in developing computers that play board games such as chess. In a game of chess, patterns are formed based on variables and values that make up the rules of the game. For example, each square of the board is a variable that is assigned a colour value. Each chess piece is also a variable which is assigned values for rank, colour and a set of legal moves.

A chess master can recognise patterns of these variables and their values without having to go through every permutation and combination of each potential move and the potential moves of the opponent. This learned knowledge of patterns is formed during hours of practice – but can be recalled instinctively and instantaneously.

In early computer development, the chess program algorithm had to assess and eliminate every possible move until the optimal choice was found. In other words, early algorithms were not based on pattern formation and pattern recognition.

Pattern formation and pattern recognition are major factors in understanding how the intelligence of the human mind is created. Any mathematical model must explain all the variables of the thought process and how they have been linked together to create an emotional pattern.

If we can teach our children how to recognise patterns of healthy, structured thinking and decision-making, the same way that we teach them how to recognise the patterns of board games like chess, then we will be teaching them the rules of the game for a mentally healthy life.

Remember, the purpose of thought is to create and automate logically accurate and emotionally healthy beliefs. Pattern formation relates to the creation of beliefs; pattern recognition relates to the automation of beliefs.

By automation I mean immediate recognition if you identify something or someone from the past without having to go through a full thought process. Automation also refers to the creation of neural networks and physiological reflexes.

10: Emotional Patterns

Let's work through the example of a fictitious life event to learn more about the variables and values that create the building blocks of our beliefs which inspire our reflexive emotional patterns. This way we can build a model for perception, independently of the Old School Model and then compare the old with the new afterwards.

Imagine witnessing a motor vehicle accident with screeching tyres and the reverberating thud of colliding heavy objects. Logical values of the life event that may become part of a dysfunctional emotional reflex may include:

- the types of sounds and/or the intensity of the sounds
- a big car dominating a small car in a physical collision
- a male driver in one car and a female driver in the other
- watching disaster unfold but being unable to stop it.

In terms of pattern formation, these logical values may inspire you emotionally to:

- be nervous around loud, noisy traffic
- become inappropriately reactive to screeching tyres

- have a sense of dread whenever you are traveling in a smaller car
- be compelled to travel by train rather than road.

In terms of generalised pattern recognition, the car accident experience may resonate with you witnessing a childhood event:

- of a loud domestic incident
- where a larger person was bullying a smaller person
- with the impending doom of being powerless to stop
- the inevitable disaster of escalating conflict.

Not all the logical elements of the life event though will be "tagged" as building blocks of a dysfunctional pattern. For example, the following logical aspects of the experience of the car wreck may not register as part of an emotional reflex:

- it was a sunny day
- it was a Tuesday
- both cars were red
- you were wearing your favourite shoes.

In the equation of the thought process, the value assigned to these logical elements is "zero", at least for that specific life event at that particular time.

11: Including All the Variables

Emotional Values

From the outset, we can agree with the Old School Model that "Emotion" is a variable to which values such as fear, dread, impending doom, nervousness, etc. can be assigned. But there can be many emotions assigned to a life event so our label in the new model will read as the plural "Emotional Values".

For those using stress-reduction and mindfulness techniques you can add a more precise dimension to an emotional value by establishing whether it is a personal emotion or conflicting personal emotions, a shared or conflicting emotion with others, or a shared or conflicting emotion with everyone in the history of the universe. The more precisely the ownership of the emotion is understood, the more precisely the unhealthy pattern can be challenged.

Logical Values

The life event also involves variables which describe what actually transpired during the experience such as the volume and types of sounds, the act of a collision, size of cars, colours, etc. A model therefore has to include "Logical Values" to which emotional values can be assigned to create a belief.

Physical Values

The life event also inspires a mechanism which physically stores the experience in the body. Obviously, the brain changes to remember the experience but at the time of a trauma, other responses, such as the fight/flight response may engage – affecting breathing, heart rate, blood pressure, digestion, temperature regulation, etc. Physical symptom and emotional memory can then merge to become one emotional pattern.

The truth is that medical diagnostic equipment is not yet sophisticated enough to detect all the physical changes that occur and become interconnected as the result of emotionality, but for the purposes of modelling let's call this variable "Physical Values". This variable accommodates all forms of physical medicine.

Electricity can pass through copper far better than it can pass through wood, as copper is far more conductive. Similarly, the intelligence of the thought process has to express itself through the physical matter of your body. The healthier your body, the more conducive your mind is to healthy thought. The variable for physical values acknowledges this relationship.

Energy Values

Eventually, artificial general intelligence will provide society with the diagnostic equipment to measure the energy, frequency and vibration of every receptor on every cell. Nikola Tesla is quoted as saying that "The day science begins to study non-physical phenomena, it will make more progress in one decade than in all the previous centuries of its existence."

Einstein also made a connection between the energetic and physical worlds with his famous formula $E=mc^2$; energy equals mass times the speed of light squared. This just means that your physical body and your energy are the same thing just in different forms.

Dog trainers often instruct dog owners to be mindful of the energy that they project to their pet. The energy that the owner projects to the dog must be consistent with the commands being given and the behaviour expected. Teaching a dog the command to sit at a busy pedestrian crossing will be less effective if the owner is projecting playful excitement.

In remembering Nikola Tesla, let's call this the variable for "Energy Values". This variable accommodates all forms of energy medicine – a component of Indigenous healing techniques worldwide.

Based on a mathematical model for human thought, it is probable that the energy, frequency and vibration of a single aspect of an unresolved trauma may be sufficient to trigger the full response of an emotional pattern. For example, the energy of being in a room with someone who is fuming with anger and repressed aggression.

Energy Values Include Light Values

Physics is not my field, but my observation of mathematics is that although the speed of light (c^2) mentioned in Einstein's $E=mc^2$ is constant, different types of light exists by virtue of its frequency and wavelength. Certain light, such as infrared light, is used for physical rehabilitation, restoring back to health the physical mass (m) and energy (E) of the living tissue.

In acknowledging the good people researching light/colour therapies as healing modalities, I have included light under the variable for energy values in my current explanation of the Fractal Perception Blueprint.

So, we have now enhanced the Old School Model of Emotions & Beliefs to a point where the building blocks of a belief and therefore an emotional pattern include emotional, logical, physical and energy values.

Fractal Perception Blueprint

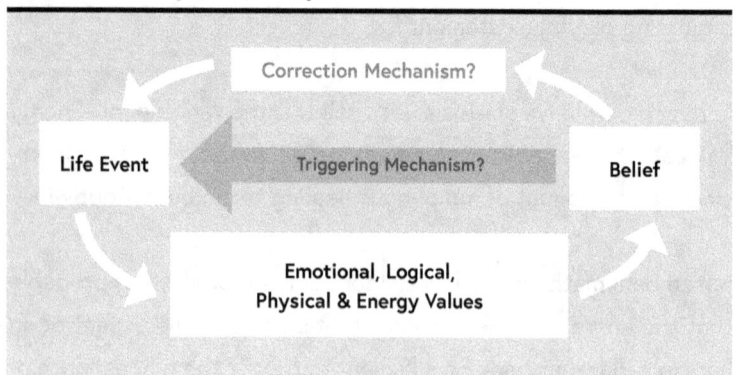

To proceed further we have to pivot. Nature and the Universe are governed by cause, effect and natural laws. To understand how our power of free will inspires self-correction we must ask, "What is the inherent design of nature?"

More specifically ...

12: What the Hell Is a Fractal?

The inherent design of nature is something called a fractal. If you have ever seen a tree, then you know what a fractal looks like. It is a simple recurring process with an ever-present, self-correction mechanism. Why this term is not taught in schools from year 1 is beyond me.

In the case of a tree, the recurring process is trunk, branch, twig, leaf. If you look at the veins within the leaf, you will see the structure of the entire tree. Turn the tree upside down and you will see that the root system mirrors the rest of the structure of the tree. If a tree grows up against the oppositional force of a fence then it will distort and change directions. The ability to self-correct is a sign of intelligence and fractal design.

Here's another good question on fractals: "How can something as complicated and unique as the human mind be explained by a series of simple, recurring steps with a self-correction mechanism?"

Let's answer a question with a question. In a game like football, you basically only do five things: pass, kick, catch, run, and tackle. So how come every game of football is different?

Well, during every play, players decide which is the best option for them personally, and the team collectively, and then act accordingly. Every play provides active players with an opportunity to influence the game to their advantage. Games can be similar but never identical.

Similarly, every thought that you have is an opportunity to move the game of life in your favour to create and automate logically accurate and emotionally healthy beliefs.

We are not trained from childhood as to what a fractal is. We therefore can't know that our thought process and the perception that it creates are fractal in design. Is it any surprise that we have a social crisis of unhealthy, unstructured thinking that escalates into a medical mental health crisis?

13: Life Lessons – Correcting Fractal Patterns

My observation from over 2 decades of attending seminars in stress-reduction techniques is that some practitioners, after finding and addressing an unhealthy belief, will intuitively also ensure that the patient is emotionally ok with not only disconnecting from the unhealthy, old belief but is also emotionally ok with adopting a preferred, new, healthy belief to replace it.

For example, unhealthy emotionality surrounding a relationship breakup may lead to a belief that relationships don't work. Whilst logical, if you are wallowing in the despair of being dumped, this logic is inaccurate and therefore unhealthy.

The healthy belief that is required to self-correct, and what I refer to as the life lesson is YES, a relationship with an incompatible partner may result in a broken heart but you are inherently lovable and you have the discernment to successfully judge partner compatibility despite their power of free will to unilaterally end the relationship at any time.

Even though you may occasionally judge poorly and despite the fact that you have the power of free will to remain petrified of relationships for the rest of your life, if you so choose.

A healthy belief does not create a life lesson – an unhealthy belief does. The variable to include in our model for perception is "Life Lesson Y/N". The decision to learn the life lesson is the ever-present self-correction mechanism in the fractal design of the human thought process.

There is an Australian expression called "passing the pub test". It describes a scenario where an average person sitting in a pub will understand an explanation because it is based on common sense. It just so happens I was alone in such an environment enjoying a pint of Guinness when I suddenly realised that the ever-present self-correction mechanism, which makes the human thought process fractal in design, is the power of free will to decide to learn the life lesson of the life event. Validate the noble, healthy belief despite what may seem to be overwhelming evidence to the contrary.

On making this realisation around 2013, I quickly Googled to see if anyone else had twigged to the idea that thought was a fractal process. I read a few different articles which didn't really hold any appeal but then I read that Ray Kurzweil, futurist and AI researcher at Google, was convinced that the thought process was fractal in design and that they were going to reverse engineer the master algorithm for thought by understanding the brain.

There have been many surprises from investigating the overlap between human health and computing. One of the biggest is the level of knowledge possessed by experts in artificial intelligence about the detailed structures of the brain.

There is a fascinating book called *The Fractal Brain Theory* by Wai H. Tsang, who has meticulously studied the hardware of the brain and physical body – right down to the level of our DNA.

His theory is that the software (algorithm for thought and perception) which inspires the hardware of our physical form is indeed fractal in design. Without knowing the algorithm, he describes some basic characteristics of what this algorithm will look like and what its basic design will be. Tsang has provided a very rudimentary description of the Fractal Mindset Blueprint.

An ability to describe something that you have never seen before is a feature of science. When the periodic table was discovered, predictions were made about the qualities, characteristics and reactivity of undiscovered elements. When these elements were eventually discovered, the predictions were incredibly accurate.

The take-home message is that the convergence of human health and computer science produces an algorithm for optimal human thought which creates an algorithm for human perception – both have the fractal design of nature and both pass the pub test.

14: Our Progress So Far!

We have managed to simplify the Old School Model of Emotions & Beliefs and established variables for logical, physical and energy values. We have also added the variable of "Life Lesson Y/N" which represents our ability to exercise free will and correct our thinking.

Fractal Perception Blueprint

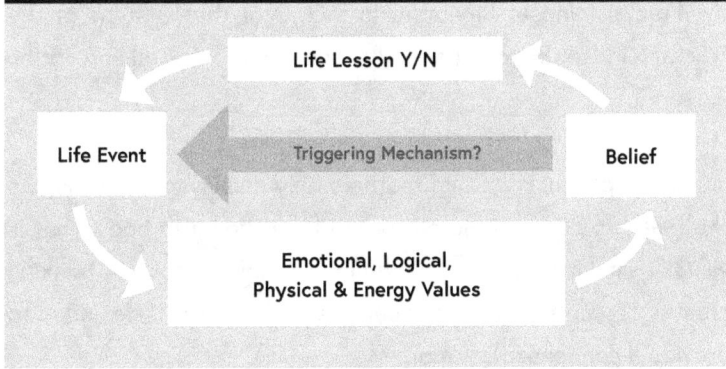

Our next challenge is to identify the triggering mechanism that inspires an unhealthy emotion to a life event. In other words, how do our beliefs explain our sensitivities and reactivities to our daily existence?

To do this we need to fully understand what beliefs are and where they come from. Because intelligence and learning are synonymous, we will call on the wisdom of the Competency Model of Learning to better understand how to learn life lessons inherent in all unhealthy beliefs and develop a Competency Model of Thinking in the process.

Two models will then be presented to demonstrate the efficiency in learning that is created by using fractal design. The first will be a non-fractal model of perception based on the Old School Model of Emotions & Beliefs. The second will be the complete Fractal Perception Blueprint itself.

A further model will illustrate how the emotional, logical, physical and energy values are the result of "calculations" made by the Fractal Mindset Blueprint. In fact, 3 of the 10 steps of the Fractal Mindset Blueprint already appear in the Fractal Perception Blueprint.

Imagine a peacock with its feathers fully displayed; now imagine the feathers being retracted to trail from the bird's body. That is visually similar to how an open mind capable of optimal thinking creates perception. It is an expansive process that is designed to provide a condensed solution.

15: Where Do Beliefs Come From?

Your beliefs are the filtered lens through which you interpret the experience of every life event: your physical, emotional, psychological and spiritual wellbeing; the achievement of your goals and aspirations; and the selection of your spouse and friends are all inspired, directly or otherwise, by your beliefs.

Similarly, recurring themes of unresolved hurt and sabotage behaviour are also the product of beliefs. Everything in your life, right down to the mood that you wake up with of a morning and share with/inflict upon those that you love, is governed by your beliefs.

You act the way that you do because of your unique combination of expectations, sensitivities and reactivities which comprise your belief systems; all of which have been created and accumulated over your lifetime by a countless number of thought processes.

Sigmund Freud, the famous Austrian neurologist who founded psychoanalysis, thought that patients could be "cured" by making conscious their subconscious thoughts. What I believe he was referring to is discovering the origins of a patient's beliefs.

So where do your beliefs come from and what types can you have?

If you have ever seen a bloodhound track down a scent over any distance, you will notice that it seems to ask a lot of questions of the territory until it locks on to the source of the scent. In this book, we are on the scent of a unifying theory of human health and computer science, so let's keep asking the right questions for the benefit of future generations who will inherit a global mental health crisis – unless we can be the catalyst of change.

Clarification by Compartmentalisation

Part of the scientific process can involve classifying subject matter into ever smaller groups to better understand their origins and therefore their interconnectedness. The classification of living organisms into genus and species, for example, means that we know that humans are different animals to the great apes, both of which are removed from kangaroos on the evolutionary tree.

Now, the simplest way to group our beliefs is to say that they are the result of nature, nurture and decision – some you are born with, some you are taught, and some you consciously or subconsciously adopt through a decision process.

Origin of Beliefs

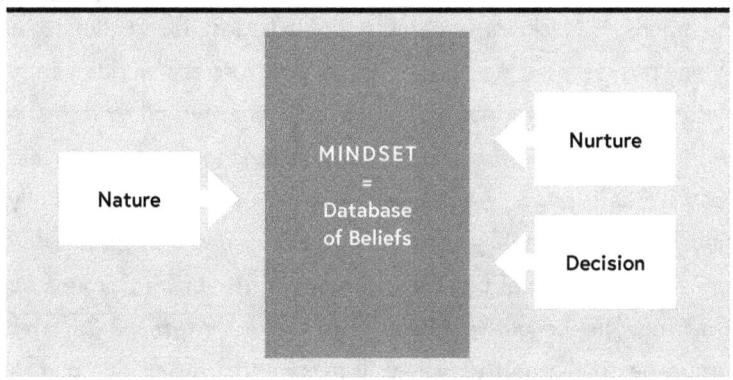

The best generic model I have seen to explain our beliefs can be developed from Maslow's Hierarchy of Needs. Abraham Maslow was an American psychologist and philosopher who theorised a tiered system that describes an upwards spiral of our wants and needs, starting with our needs to physically survive and ending with what he describes as self-actualisation.

That is, we deserve to have the basic needs of physical sustenance and safety met. We deserve the right to love, to be loved and to love ourselves. We deserve the right to blossom into our full potential.

The right to have these needs satisfied is what I refer to as our noble healthy beliefs. Having any of these rights compromised can create an unhealthy emotional response and therefore an unhealthy belief which in turn creates a life lesson. Logically understanding the origins of a belief, helps you to validate the noble healthy belief that has been compromised, and detach from unhealthy emotionality – thereby learning the life lesson.

So, let the bloodhound in you off the leash and let's keep asking questions. If Maslow's Hierarchy of Needs describes beliefs that we all possess, is it possible that we come into the world already with life lessons to learn? Is it possible that we come into the world with a free pass and never have to endure particular life lessons? Is it possible that there are life lessons that our family line has to continually repeat until one generation breaks the unhealthy emotional pattern? Do people attract into groups so that they can collectively learn or repeat a life lesson? Can this group be so big as to involve all humanity? Can all this human interaction occur and still preserve the right of each individual to exercise the power of free will?

I have a motto, that "when in doubt, listen to clever people!" Technology is all about converging and integrating information into one seamless database of knowledge, so let's combine the contributions of Maslow, an advanced theory of genetics, spiritual texts and our collective responsibility to each other and arrive at a more expansive model for the origin of our beliefs.

Origin of Beliefs

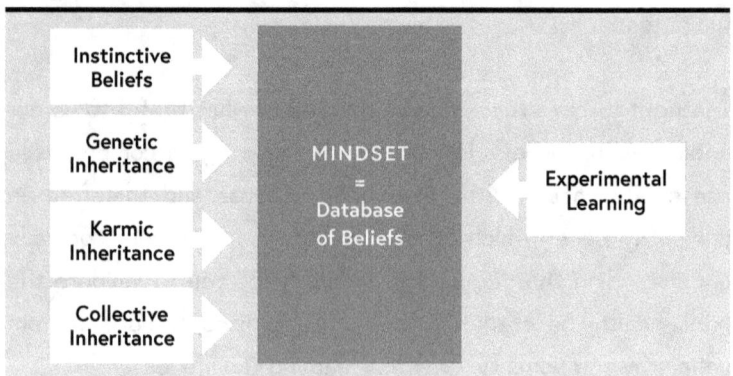

As well as providing insight to your personal mindset, the aim of this book is to also help you understand the mindset of people who you may be trying to help or influence – but don't really understand. If any of the above categories of belief don't resonate with your thinking, in terms of a mathematical model, then assign a value of zero to it – despite the fact that someone else may place a much higher value on that category.

In the words of F. Scott Fitzgerald, "the test of a first-rate intelligence is the ability to hold two opposed ideas in the mind at the same time, and still retain the ability to function."

16: Types of Beliefs

Instinctive Beliefs

These beliefs, as described by Maslow, are the beliefs that we naturally come into the world with and share in various shapes and forms with every human being in the history of the Universe. For example, we all share the need for physical sustenance from food and drink. We share a tolerance range of levels for temperature, atmosphere oxygenation, radiation, immunity to disease, etc.

In this category of beliefs, there are no pre-existing life lessons of any consequence to learn. This may change as our life progresses by virtue of the unhealthy decisions we make.

For example, someone may come into the world with an instinctive ability to accumulate wealth, but if they begin to validate themselves based on material possessions and devalue those who place less emphasis on monetary gain, then there is a life lesson to learn from this.

Alternatively, they may have come into the world with deeper issues of self-worth from genetic or karmic inheritance and their intelligence has combined beliefs of wealth and self-worth to highlight the life lesson of the deeper issue.

Remember we don't do things unless we benefit. An over-riding benefit is always to have a life lesson brought to our attention. The mind/body complex is perfectly designed to repeat life lessons until they are learned. There is a difference of course between a gentle reminder and being beaten into submission. Intelligence includes the ability to reflect and correct – the quicker the better!

Genetic Inheritance

This classification relates to beliefs that have been handed down via the genetics of either or both parental lines. There is a field of research called epigenetics. Put very simply, epigenetics is how the neurophysiology of our chemical soup can influence our genetic expression in a way that can be inherited by future generations. A major component of our chemical soup, of course, is our emotionality which creates or re-enforces our beliefs.

Epigenetics deals not only with the inherited legacy of trauma but also with the legacy of emotional resilience. In nature, the same mechanism which creates function can also create dysfunction. The reality is that we don't know what proportion of our belief systems have a genetic component.

If you have a life lesson that you share with either parent then entertain the possibility that there is a genetic component to it. If that realisation makes you drop to the floor, rocking in the foetal position wailing, "Oh no! I've become my mother/father!", I'd be suspecting genetic inheritance.

In stress management/mindfulness techniques there is a difference in conceptualising an unhealthy personal emotion, compared to an unhealthy emotion that is shared with an entire genetic line and potentially risking the quality of life of offspring if it remains unresolved. Ending intergenerational trauma means dealing with life lessons relating to genetic inheritance.

Karmic Inheritance

The idea of karmic inheritance evolved from spiritual texts of Hinduism, Buddhism, etc. It relates to the concept of reincarnation, where the soul continually returns to the physical form in the quest for "enlightenment". Lessons to be learned in this life are determined by beliefs, actions and decisions of previous lives.

As indicated, if you don't believe in reincarnation then the value that you assign to this variable in a mathematical model for the thought process is zero. Are there past lives? I can't answer that question, but the prospect of returning to a world that we create in this life certainly has the sting of a brand of humour that seems suspiciously like natural justice.

For those that are open to karmic inheritance, the aim in stress management/mindfulness techniques is to create a story that mirrors the storyline surrounding a current unhealthy belief – or is exactly the opposite.

For example, an inability to forgive a former partner for the hurt caused by infidelity may mirror an unsuccessful relationship in a past life where you were the victim of a similar trauma. It may also be that you were the perpetrator of infidelity causing emotional trauma to someone else in a past life. Experiencing the logic and emotion of both sides of a life event may provide deeper perspective in normalising an unhealthy belief.

The debate as to whether reincarnation exists or not is not the focus. Committing to an understanding that a powerful story can balance the logical, emotional, physical and energy values of a mathematical formula for human thought is the life changing, take-home message.

Collective Inheritance

Each generation faces challenges that are either unresolved by previous generations or are the result of change in their lifetime. For example, raiding neighbouring villages to steal the livestock and carry off the women folk is not the common occurrence that it once was – collectively we have evolved beyond that practice.

Sanitation, slavery, colonial rule, Indigenous rights, a social security system, freedom of information, cyber security – these are all examples of lessons that we, as the apex species on the planet, have had to consider in order to progress as a cohesive global collective, with varying levels of failure and success.

The progression of machine learning to a point where it mirrors or exceeds human intelligence is possibly the biggest collective inheritance humanity will face in this generation. Technology collectively challenges whether advancement will be used for the common good or used to divide society. As Nikola Tesla famously said, "Science is but a perversion of itself unless it has as its ultimate goal the betterment of humanity."

Shared emotions and shared beliefs create a shared consciousness. Every time that you communicate with yourself or someone else it creates a consciousness. The biggest current challenge to our collective consciousness is the subject of this book: what is the purpose of human thought?

The answer of how to create and ethically implement "true" artificial intelligence and the solution to the global mental health crisis are the same thing. Our ability to learn the life lessons presented by these challenges will determine how enslaved future generations are to technology and to their own mental health.

Experiential Learning

How and what we learn from playing the game of life is what could be classed as experiential learning. The most effective way to play any game is to begin by knowing the rules of the game and how to execute them.

Because the mind/body complex is perfectly designed to repeat life lessons, unhealthy emotional reflexes fire in response to the pattern recognition of an unhealthy belief. People who are less mindful and self-aware will aimlessly repeat life lessons, becoming increasingly adamant that others should change to alleviate their inconvenience or that an emotional challenge is unsolvable.

People who are on a journey of self-discovery will be far more inclined to reflect and correct – changing what they can and accepting what they can't, but without devaluing any aspect of the life experience. Please note that there is a difference between assigning an appropriate value to some aspect of a life event and devaluing it.

A devaluation involves an unhealthy emotion, creating an unhealthy belief and an ongoing spiral of life lessons. Assigning an appropriate value means seeing something for what it is and moving forward in the knowledge that you will never receive an explanation, apology or any form of compensation for having endured the life event.

The more that you can be mindful of your noble healthy beliefs when playing the game of life, the more that you can "play what is in front of you"; neutralising the stimulus of an unhealthy thought in the same way that a martial artist would neutralise the stimulus of a physical assault.

17: Shock and Awe

A mathematical model for human thought brings a new perspective to the role that the expectations of our beliefs play in creating emotional reflexes and neurological patterns.

Our beliefs inspire how we view the world. More specifically, they provide an expectation of how we perceive or prefer the world to be in the past, present or future. Life events might fail to reach our expectations or they may exceed our expectations.

For example, I might walk out of an exam at school totally convinced that my grade will be between 60% to 80%. In other words, the tolerance range of my belief is between 60 and 80 out of 100 – that is the expected value. A grade of more than 80% will inspire surprise ranging to awe; less than 60% will inspire surprise ranging to shock.

To clarify terminology for the purposes of this book, any belief that is exceeded in a perceived beneficial way we will call awe. Any belief that is exceeded in a perceived negative way we will call shock. Any life event that falls within the tolerance range of a belief we will call expected. Clearly, we are not using the term shock in the context of the medical condition.

My observation is that the biggest challenges to our emotional health can come when we are totally blindsided by a life event. Thought is a problem-solving exercise; being blindsided initially represents what is effectively a failure to compute! It's as though the cogs of your brain temporarily grind to a near halt and then gradually restore momentum as your mind begins to form stories that explain how to perceive the life event.

In the process of restoring momentum, I believe that the mind can be more prone to associating unhealthy emotions to the life event. A death by accident, a friend's suicide with no forewarning of mental distress, discovering as an adult that you are adopted, an unforeseen divorce or infidelity, a violent, random assault – these are all examples of a life event by which you can be totally blindsided, leaving you more prone to unhealthy emotionality.

Sure, had you been asked before the life event whether such a thing could possibly happen, you would have acknowledged that it could; but it was so far beyond the realms of the expected possibility that it was not even worth entertaining – but then it happened! So, room on the extremities of the scale of shock must also be made for being blindsided.

Similarly, you can also be blindsided by awe. For example, winning the lottery, escaping a potentially fatal situation unscathed, unexpectedly meeting the love of your life, or waking from a terrifying nightmare to realise that it was only a dream.

The Shock and Awe of a Belief

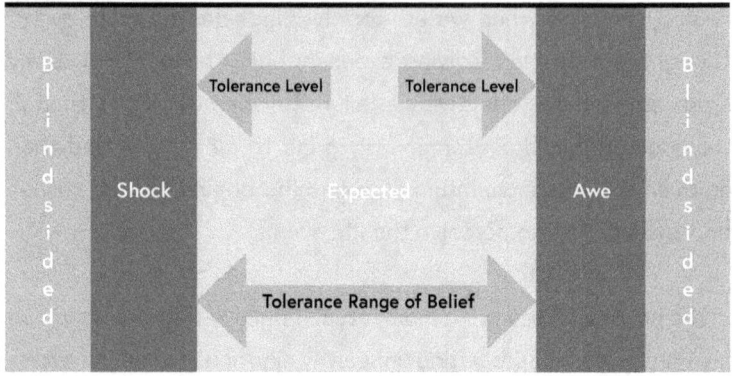

There are several reasons why it is important to understand the full spectrum of your tolerance levels to a life event. Firstly, the aim is to be emotionally ok and balanced in all aspects of your life. That means changing what you can and accepting what you can't, but not devaluing any aspect of the experience. That includes the full spectrum of possibilities of the life event even if they involve being blindsided, shocked or awed.

Secondly, humans seem to have an inherent trait that as soon as something negative happens, they subconsciously wish that it had never happened and could be undone or reversed. We have an innate ability to comprehend the full spectrum of possibilities of a life event but create unhealthy emotionality when our preference is denied us. It's as though we go into a sulking process of continually comparing the negative to the positive of what could have been.

Conversely, if we are blindsided by a life event where something extremely positive comes into our lives, we can hold vulnerabilities about losing it.

This is where stress-reduction/mindful techniques may assist to broaden the tolerance range of the belief to include the entire spectrum of possibilities of the life event from the blindsiding and shocking to the ecstasy of the awesomeness of negative aspects magically being reversed – and any eventuality on the spectrum in between.

Thirdly, and possibly most importantly for understanding emotional patterns, being blindsided can become a life event in its own right, which can be subconsciously generalised, exaggerated and catastrophised to create logical, emotional, physical and energy values of an unhealthy belief that fire every subsequent time you are blindsided by any life event at any time in the future.

In other words, an unhealthy emotional response to the shock of being blindsided can become a generalised, systemic flaw in your thinking – every time that you are blindsided.

For example, being conceived out of wedlock in the Western world at one stage was considered to be an absolute cultural taboo. Questions of how the mother would cope emotionally and financially ran a distant second to the shame and moral judgement she was subjected to. I've heard many stories of mothers falling pregnant and being so blindsided and shocked that they have spent weeks in bed trying to come to terms with their unexpected predicament.

I met a member of an elite combat unit who relayed that his mother was blindsided in this manner when she fell pregnant with him. I told him that as counterintuitive as this may seem, coming into the physiology of his mother's chemical soup of extreme distress and shock like that at conception may mean that he is hypersensitive or over-reactive to unexpected life events.

His response was that he knew exactly what I was talking about and added that the challenge of overcoming that hyper-sensitivity and reactivity in an affirmative, strategic way rather than "freezing in shock" to an unexpected life event was one of the things that he loved most about his professional training.

This example highlights that healing and learning are the same thing – both are exercises in empowerment through humility. The key is to have the self-awareness or mindfulness to identify that there is something in your life which is unhealthy or "not working for you" and choosing to do something about it – namely learn the life lesson.

The decision to reflect and correct to learn the life lesson is no different to learning any other knowledge base or skillset. You have to challenge what you are currently doing and challenge what you currently think that you know. As Einstein once said, "The definition of insanity is doing the same thing over and over again, but expecting a different result."

Let's investigate some practical applications of how the shock and awe of a belief can be used to better understand your mindset before expanding further on the concept that learning and healing are the same thing with separate models for competent learning and competent thinking.

18: Tolerance Range of a Belief

The tolerance range of a belief determines our sensitivities and reactivities to the stimulus of a life event. It is a fundamental building block of an emotional pattern and as such plays a vital role in developing effective protocols for the use of stress-reduction/mindfulness techniques.

As a preview to the Thought Martial Arts online courses, let's look at three examples of how the tolerance range of a belief can be used in your self-development work to highlight areas of improvement in your mindset.

Perfectionism

No discussion on the tolerance range of our beliefs would be complete without addressing our potentially unhealthy relationship with perfection. Perfectionism tells us that if we are not perfect then we are somehow "less than" and a failure – maybe even to the point of being unlovable or unworthy! We are either brilliant or broken; hero or loser.

Perfectionism is an extremely draining mental practice. Subconsciously, even achieving 99.99% is unacceptable – it means that we are not trying hard enough. Should we achieve 100%, a celebration is out of the question because starting at 0% on the next task immediately becomes the focus. There is no tolerance range to the belief because there is only one tolerance level and that is 100%.

A further complication is added to the mix if we expect perfection in others!

Tolerance Range of Perfectionism

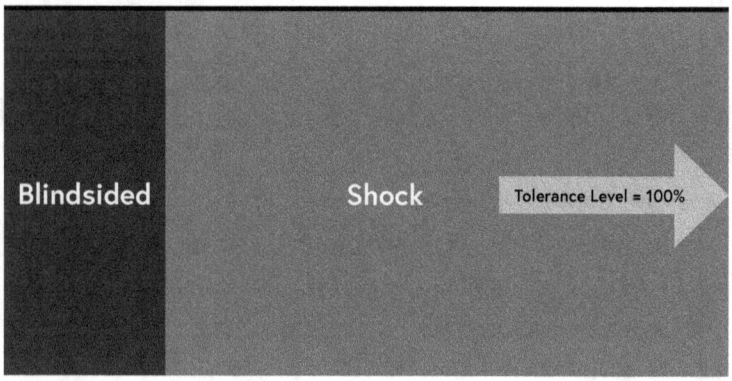

But we don't do things unless we benefit. The perceived benefit of perfection is that it solves some type of problem. If you are perfect then you, or someone that you love, can feel perfectly safe, perfectly loved, perfectly happy, etc.

The aim of stress-reduction/mindfulness techniques is to establish and reduce the unhealthy emotional reflex that inspires the unhealthy belief that perfectionism is an effective strategy to deal with life events.

Enlightenment

The focus of the artificial intelligence industry is in understanding optimal human thought. They have an advantage over psychology in this department because they program in the logic of computer language and don't have to factor in emotionality. Please note that programming machines to possess the illusion of emotionality is a separate issue.

No unhealthy emotionality means that all decisions are logically based, which for modelling purposes means no unhealthy beliefs, no life lessons and a tolerance range of 100%. We are therefore looking at a mathematical model for enlightenment.

Tolerance Range of 'Enlightenment'

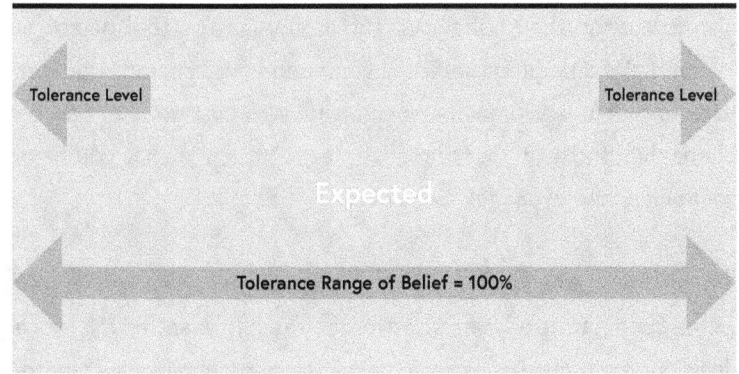

Because the mind is a time machine, we can now challenge our mindset with questions such as, "If I was currently enlightened and with the benefit of hindsight, what would I change about my reaction to that specific life event?" Alternatively, "If I was enlightened at the time of that life event, how would my reaction have been different?"

Are Your Expectations Realistic?

The tolerance range for every belief that you have inspires your emotional response to every life event that you experience. Your sensitivities and reactivities inspire the assignment of emotional, logical, physical and energy values in the equation of your thought processes.

I've lost track of the number of times that as a patient in my own self-development work, I've spent a lot of time using stress-reduction/mindfulness techniques on a life event that's been bothering me, only to realise that the tolerance range of my belief that inspired the emotional response to begin with was profoundly unrealistic.

For example, you may have a belief that you can influence someone else to change their behaviour. The reality may be that person is incapable of changing their behaviour and your influence equates to zero. But every time that person fails to change, you can be blindsided because your unrealistic expectation is that you have some influence over their behaviour.

A realistic expectation is that individuals are given the power of free will to conduct themselves however they see fit, even though those decisions may cause us extreme pain, discomfort and inconvenience.

Part 3
A Recurring Theme

The Quest for a Competent Mind

19: Competency Model of Learning

Learning and Healing Are the Same Thing!

To further explore the connection between learning and healing, we'll defer to the Competency Model of Learning – yet another model that can be used with stress-reduction/mindfulness techniques to better access the building blocks of the thought process which creates belief.

We've established that an unhealthy belief creates a life lesson. Learning that life lesson involves restoring faith in a noble healthy belief, despite evidence – possibly overwhelming evidence – to the contrary. So, what do we already know about the learning process from educators and teachers that we might apply to learning life lessons?

In corporate training, there is something called the Competency Model of Learning, originally developed by Martin M. Broadwell, which explains a 4-step progression from not knowing that a knowledge base or skillset even exists to adopting it as second nature.

These steps are:

1. Unconscious Incompetence – you don't even know what you don't know.

2. Conscious Incompetence – you now know what you previously didn't know and recognise a need to know more.

3. Conscious Competence – with focus comes knowledge and a demonstrated ability.

4. Unconscious Competence – knowledge and ability are second nature.

Competency Model of Learning

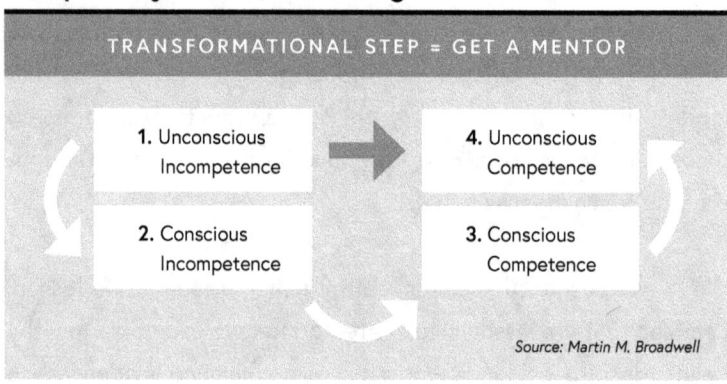

Source: Martin M. Broadwell

As an example, the idea that the human thought process could be a natural law and algorithm is a totally alien concept to most people. A totally new concept represents step 1 of the Competency Model. A desire to learn more and read this book represents a progression to step 2, conscious incompetence. Studying this book and possibly even enrolling in the associated online courses to integrate the theory with stress-reduction and mindfulness techniques will create step 3, conscious competence. With focus and commitment over time to the theory and practice of available knowledge on this subject, you will move to step 4 of the Competency Model, unconscious competence.

With stress-reduction and mindfulness techniques, unhealthy emotionality can be challenged at each step of the Competency Model of Learning. For example, someone's reluctance to challenge their mindset concerning a recurring unhealthy emotional pattern that they know stems from a traumatic experience from childhood means that they are stuck on step 2 of the learning process, conscious incompetence.

They are aware that the trauma and recurring unhealthy pattern exists but are not convinced of the need to learn more – probably for many reasons, all of them valid. The unhealthy emotionality surrounding this trauma may relate to the fact that they will never receive justice for what transpired – so why dwell on it?

The life lesson would then revolve around being emotionally ok that they will never receive the natural justice of an explanation, apology or any form of compensation. It may also involve an acceptance that people have the power of free will to conduct themselves how they choose – even though it may be at our expense.

Part of the life lesson is to broaden the tolerance range of the belief to include both extremities of the spectrum of the life event. Yes – some children have to go through that type of trauma and are blindsided when their noble healthy beliefs of their right to safety and love are compromised. Others have an ideal childhood – and there is the spectrum between ideal and blindsided by trauma. Being emotionally ok with the spectrum of possibilities, despite the fact that you have a preference, is a vital part of learning the life lesson.

The reality is that what happened has happened and the child can move forward knowing that they will never receive natural justice – changing what they can and accepting what they can't, but without devaluing any aspect of the experience. Placing them in a position where they can progress to becoming unconsciously competent at dealing with that specific childhood trauma.

The Competency Model of Learning is a very valuable tool when used with stress-reduction/mindfulness techniques to address the full spectrum of the blindsiding, shock and awe of a life event. To be blindsided equates to being unconsciously incompetent – you didn't know what you didn't know.

As an aside, the most effective way to fast track the learning process is to find a mentor – someone who has already been through the entire learning process and can help you find short-cuts to progress from unconscious incompetence to unconscious competence. They can also objectively identify personal strengths and weaknesses to which you may be oblivious.

20: Competency Model of Thinking

Disempowerment to Empowerment – The Power of Patterns

The Competency Model of Learning shows a path to learning the life lesson. To progress from one step to the next you have the power of free will to change from being the disempowered victim of your circumstance to becoming the empowered victim. The term "victim" is used simply to describe someone who has experienced a life event – it is not a devaluing description.

Unconscious incompetence equates to being blindsided by a life event that was well outside the tolerance range of a belief. By progressively moving through the stages of the Competency Model, you arrive at a state of being where the life lesson is second nature and you are unconsciously competent at assigning logically accurate and emotionally healthy beliefs to the life event.

But your mind is a time machine that has an ability to conceptualise anything humanly possible from your past, present or future. Anything that is conceptualised consciously or otherwise becomes a new life event to which emotional, logical, physical and energy values of a belief can be assigned. This means that a belief relating to a life event can be updated every time that it is conceptualised. This update can be healthy or unhealthy.

There is a concept in machine learning called "backpropagation", which is how computer programs take new information and use it to enhance and improve the accuracy of predictions made by the software. It's effectively a pattern-enhancing, background learning function.

For example, if you have ever shopped online, your customer profile and purchasing history is run through an algorithm and you will be presented with a list of products that are predicted to be of interest to you. At one stage an irate father in the USA complained to a well-known retail company about the inappropriateness of maternity products being advertised to his 14-year-old daughter. The father later apologised as the buying patterns identified by the algorithm were even more accurate than the mental connections made by loving parental supervision.

Backpropagation means that a Competency Model of Thinking must extend beyond the unconscious competence of learning an individual life lesson to an ability to correct systemic flaws in the interconnected beliefs of our mindset. I refer to this step as Integrative Competence.

Also, the Competency Model of Learning does not reflect the reality that once a life lesson is learned, it is imperative that that information be passed on so that others can benefit from the knowledge or skillset. Being emotionally ok with teaching others is what I refer to as Collective Competence.

So we can now expand on Martin M. Broadwell's Competency Model of Learning to create a Competency Model of Thinking.

Competency Model of Thinking

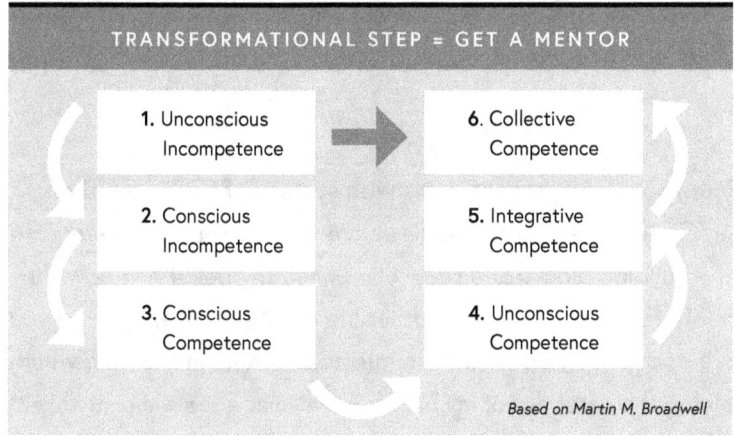

Based on Martin M. Broadwell

21: Integrative Competence

Integrative competence deals with systemic flaws in our thought processes. These systemic flaws are identified by understanding the building blocks of a particular unhealthy belief and how they relate to the life lessons of other life events. Effectively what you are asking is, "In learning the mistakes of this life lesson, where else in the database of my beliefs have I made the same mistake?"

The artificial intelligence industry is always trying to correct past errors and enhance future processing. The focus is always on optimal function. Humans by virtue of their power of free will and emotional reflexes, established from conception and possibly prior, are not so lucky.

On the positive side, we have an ability to create healthy beliefs relating to the present and future. We also have the intelligence to recall life events of the past and pursue a healthy agenda to reflect and correct unhealthy beliefs. But intelligence is a double-edged sword.

What if your mind can have an unhealthy agenda behind recalling life events of the past? What if that unhealthy agenda is to rewrite history to validate a current, strongly-held, unhealthy belief – the equivalent of an unhealthy backpropagation? This means that if we are not mindful, we can systematically corrupt our database of beliefs of the past, present and future with interconnecting, invalidating unhealthy beliefs.

Mathematically, this is possible and, based on the current social crisis of unhealthy unstructured thinking, I'd suggest more than probable. For example, a teenager who feels that they don't fit in at home or school might ruminate for hours with storytelling of how inadequate they are or how no-one acknowledges or accepts them for who they are; thereby validating their theory of social inadequacy and invalidating any prior life events that could disprove that theory.

By identifying the mechanism by which dysfunction was created, we also have the mechanism to attempt to reverse that dysfunction – healthy backpropagation! The aim then being to systematically enhance in a healthy way the database of our beliefs of the past, present and future using stress-reduction, mindfulness and healing techniques.

This is why having a mathematical model to teach our kids how to think is so important. It also provides a street map for the stress-reduction, mindfulness and healing techniques which are like the street sweepers of emotional debris. Understanding the building blocks of the thought process enables us to identify patterns of systemic flaws in our mindset.

The ability to retrospectively examine whether your expectations for a specific life event were realistic and then challenge all your beliefs as to whether they are realistic, is a further example of integrative competence.

For example, someone may have very fixed opinions on a specific topic and are incapable of seeing another person's point of view. It's often referred to as having a "black and white" opinion. If this person has "black and white" opinions on all their beliefs, this represents a systemic flaw of inflexible thinking.

If they are compelled to have a "black and white" opinion on topics they haven't researched then there is a tendency to provide expert opinions on things they know nothing about. They can be opinionated, stubborn and decidedly poor company. There is nothing wrong with being stubborn – so long as you are right!

The objective is then to identify how the person benefits emotionally from holding systemic "black and white" opinions or alternatively why flexible thinking may be emotionally unpalatable, using stress-reduction/mindfulness techniques to reduce unhealthy emotionality where appropriate.

For example, someone who validates their self-worth based on the attention of others may subconsciously be indifferent as to whether that attention is positive or negative. So long as they are the centre of attention, they feel good about themselves. "Black and white" opinions can certainly attract attention, hence the emotional benefit!

The focus of stress-reduction/mindfulness techniques would revolve around the need for external validation from others rather than the inflexibility of the opinions held.

But there is a further step that we can take in becoming a competent thinker. Personally, I believe that the purpose of our existence is to deal with the emotionality of our personal life lessons so that we are better placed to help others learn theirs. This is why I believe so firmly that the future of society lies in the hands of self-aware and well-intentioned people – they are best placed and more predisposed to help others.

The ability to learn the life lesson of a life event to the extent that you are prepared to help others is what I refer to as ...

22: Collective Competence

Shared emotions and shared beliefs create a shared group consciousness. Shared healthy beliefs create a healthy group consciousness; shared unhealthy beliefs create a shared unhealthy consciousness.

If you have ever seen the dressing room celebration of a Super Bowl-winning franchise of the American National Football League, then you will understand the concept of the energy of a group consciousness of success. Alternatively, if you have ever attended a child's funeral, you will understand the group consciousness of people bound by the energy of grief and the compassion for surviving parents and family.

Every time that you have an intention towards another person, or communicate with another person, it creates a consciousness that is formed by the energy, frequency and vibration of the emotional, logical and physical values of the thought process. Understanding that knowledge can change the way that you interact with people.

More importantly, every time that you communicate with yourself it creates your personal consciousness; the consciousness that you must endure 24/7 in the body that is maintained by that same consciousness. Einstein reminds us that physical mass and energy are just different forms of the same thing.

Collective competence involves an understanding that you have an ability to influence the world in a positive way – but you have to be emotionally ok or congruent with sharing the wisdom of your own life lessons for the betterment of others. The healthiest way to honour your suffering is to ensure that others don't have to endure a similar suffering.

But you can't give away what you don't have. Giving with the disproportionate expectation of some reward or recognition is not emotionally healthy for the giver or receiver. Helping others benefit from your life experiences and knowledge while you have outstanding emotionality on the subject matter can trigger unhealthy emotional reflexes with varying degrees of consequences to your health.

This doesn't mean that you should avoid striving for collective competence. What it means is that the more you give, the more you have to be emotionally ok with what you are giving and emotionally ok with the currency of the exchange. That currency can vary from financial to altruistic, but the exchange must be mutually beneficial.

My strongest recommendation for people who have progressed to a level of collective competence is to be vigilant of your own mindset and emotional triggers. To maintain the level of performance that you wish to achieve, without detracting from your own health, you have to tend to your own garden first and foremost – because the world needs you!

23: A Competent Mind

The aim of the thought process is to learn and remember/create and automate beliefs about the world in which we live. We progress from not knowing something to knowing it.

A competent mind will take that progression further to identify similar patterns of knowledge and establish a connection between associated information. This process of integrative competence is involved with the practice of lateral thinking and the concept of backpropagation in machine-learning.

Using the above model, the final challenge for a competent mind is to be emotionally congruent with sharing the learned knowledge and experience with others – collective competence.

Following is a diagram highlighting in general terms how the Competency Model of Thinking follows a similar pattern to the Fractal Perception Blueprint. I appreciate that there are inconsistencies in this approach but I include this model as an overview, particularly for visual learners.

The Quest for a Competent Mind

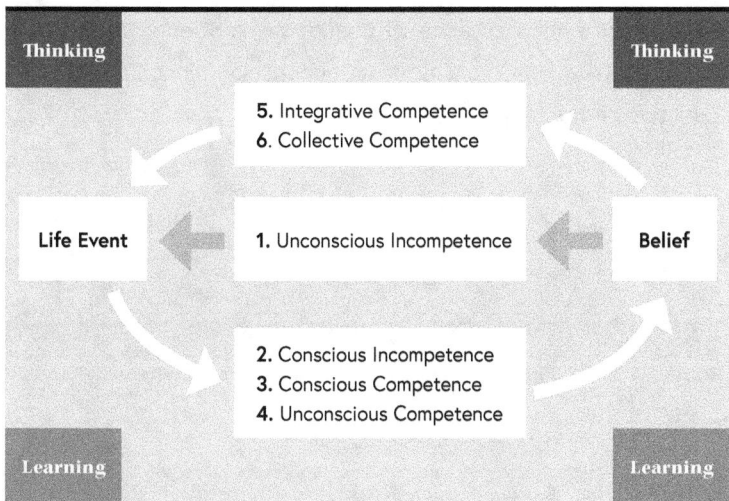

Our beliefs inspire how we interpret the life event. Unconscious incompetence challenges the competent mind with the question "Have I seen this life event before?" and challenges the tolerance range of our existing knowledge and beliefs.

The assignment of emotional, logical, physical and energy values occurs as we progress from conscious incompetence to unconscious incompetence – thereby creating a belief.

As the thought process progresses to integrative competence, any pattern contained within a belief will be cross-referenced to other beliefs and updated. The competent mind is then challenged to be emotionally ok with sharing the learned knowledge through collective competence.

Any model for the human thought process can be used with stress-reduction, mindfulness and healing techniques. There is a protocol for the quest for a competent mind in the Thought Martial Arts online courses to challenge emotional congruence with the task of progressing from unconscious incompetence to collective competence.

Part 4
The Love Story

**Perception Completes Thought
While Logic and Emotion Wave**

24: Modelling the New Information

My greatest hope for this work is for it to be taught to school kids from a very early age. To do this we need a very succinct illustration that pulls this new-found information together in an easily digestible way.

So let's detail our progress so far.

1. Apart from using the plural for the emotions variable, we have identified the other variables to which values are assigned and their significance to the integrity of a model for perception – i.e., logical, physical and energy values.

2. We have identified the mechanism by which we exercise the power of free will to reflect and correct an unhealthy belief – i.e., the life lesson.

3. We have identified the triggering mechanism to explain what inspires an unhealthy emotion to a life event i.e., the tolerance range of a belief.

To highlight the simplicity of fractal design, let's first illustrate all the variables of perception that we've identified using the outdated paradigm design of the Old School Model of Emotions & Beliefs.

Old School Model Structure for Perception

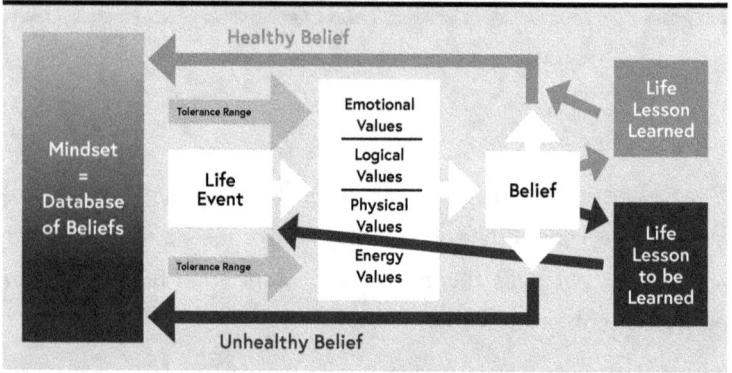

Even though the above diagram contains all the variables of perception, it is extremely cumbersome and doesn't readily lend itself to healthy structured thinking.

From the above illustration, though, please note the variables for emotional values, logical values, physical values and energy values are in separate, distinct boxes. Another feature is that a life lesson learned is treated differently to a life lesson *to be* learned. These two points will be addressed after the Fractal Perception Blueprint is presented.

Fractal Perception Blueprint

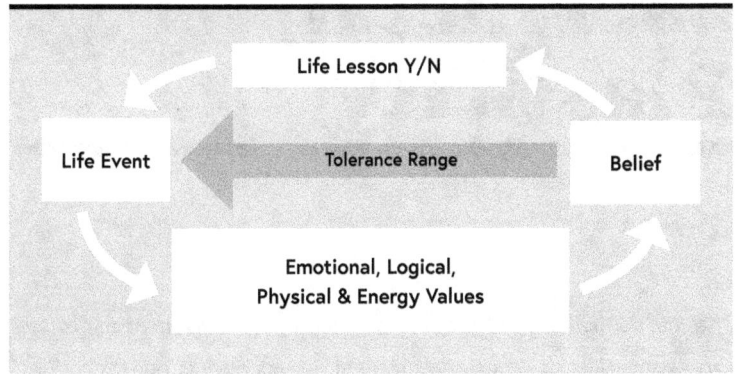

The above model for the Fractal Perception Blueprint is a simple recurring process, with an ever-present self-correction mechanism. It includes all the necessary variables to create perception. It also creates a variable for "Life Lesson Y/N" rather than the clutter caused by representing them as two separate values in the illustration for the Old School Model Structure for Perception.

The life lesson becomes a new life event in the recurring thought process – even though it may be a subconscious one that is never consciously identified or addressed. It still, however, affects mindset and behaviour.

25: Fractal Plasticity

The most striking difference between the two models is the representation of emotional, logical, physical and energy values. Including these variables in an open box represents the reality of the interconnectedness of the human condition; emotionally, logically, physically and energetically.

A characteristic of neurology is something called neuroplasticity, which simply means "nerves that fire together, wire together". The intelligence of the body is asking, "What neurological connections can I make to reinforce what I have learned?" This phenomenon is used extensively in rehabilitating the nervous system after physical injury.

But neuroplasticity is also a key factor in the dysfunctional patterns formed when the body is injured. The nervous system controls every cell and every system of the body. The open box in the in the above Fractal Perception Blueprint means that emotional, logical, physical and energetic values are free to interact and connect in any way that the mind and body has the potential to achieve. I refer to this phenomenon as "Fractal Plasticity".

Currently, both in science and society in general, there is a growing view that when it comes to health, stress can cause just about anything. In years gone by there was a tendency to dismiss stress-related symptoms as psychosomatic.

In medicine, "idiopathic" is a term which simply means that the cause or origin of an illness or condition is unknown or not fully understood. It is commonly used throughout medical diagnosis reference books. Fractal plasticity allows for a model where any physical or energetic sign or symptom can theoretically be linked to the human thought process – conscious or otherwise.

The Fractal Perception Blueprint converges physical and energetic medicine with the purpose of thought which is to create and automate logically accurate and emotionally healthy beliefs. Fractal plasticity therefore enables an advanced philosophical model of health which is far more convergent and integrated than what is currently provided by a traditional university education in this field.

26: An Advanced Philosophical Model of Health

The progressive introduction of artificial general intelligence (AGI) will scrutinise all known human knowledge for any type of interconnectedness or similarity and present a unified database of facts and relationships.

Human health will be transformed by a level of diagnostic imaging that is difficult to comprehend based on today's technology. Despite the best intentions and validating science of all forms of medicine, there will be a convergence of medical knowledge to present a far more integrated and holistic understanding of how the body functions. Let's pre-empt the arrival of AGI and offer a philosophical model of health based on what is already generally accepted in different fields of human science.

Over 5000 years of Traditional Chinese Medicine (TCM) teaches us that pairs of muscles are associated with organs; two of the stabilising muscles of the knee, for example, relate to the gall bladder. TCM also teaches that emotions are associated with organs; for example, the liver/gall bladder relates to anger and resentment.

Neurology teaches us that nerves supply every cell in the body, and physiology teaches us that there are receptors for "molecules of emotion" on every cell. Epigenetics teaches that emotionality can change the way in which DNA expresses itself and this change can be passed to future generations. Psychology teaches us that unhealthy emotionality can cause intrusive thoughts and avoidance behaviours.

Wai H. Tsang, in his book *The Fractal Brain Theory*, teaches that the hardware of the human body is fractal in design. The Fractal Mindset Blueprint teaches that the human thought process and the perception that it creates are fractal algorithms and mathematical models.

So, combining this knowledge means that there is a fractal design to the entire mind/body complex whereby muscles, joints, organs, every cell, our DNA, the entire nervous system, intrusive thoughts and avoidance behaviour are all linked by fractal algorithms and mathematical models for the human thought process and the perception that it creates.

27: Thought Creates Perception

Mathematical equations create values. The Fractal Mindset Blueprint is a 10-step model/equation/algorithm which calculates the emotional, logical, physical and energy values of the Fractal Perception Blueprint. More specifically, the calculation takes place at steps 2 to 8 of the thought process as illustrated in the below model.

The life event of step 1, the belief in step 9, and the "Life Lesson Y/N" in step 10 are features of the full thought process and the perception that it creates.

Fractal Perception to Fractal Mindset

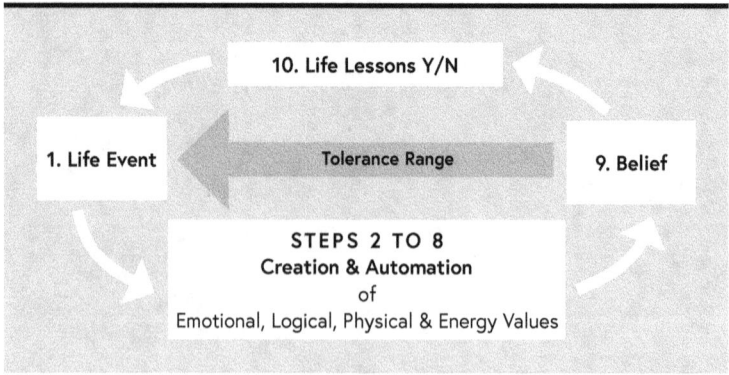

The next chapters will explain how a formula for the human thought process reduces and condenses to a model for perception – the same way that a peacock reduces and condenses its feathers after displaying full plumage.

28: Fractal Mindset Blueprint

Fractal Sequence

The schoolyard game of hopscotch is always the simplest analogy to explain how the thought process works. In hopscotch, if you step outside a landing zone then you have to start the process again until you can navigate each landing zone, from start to finish, without error.

Similarly, the thought process can be thought of as a game involving a sequential series of steps, each step representing a state of mind. Associating an unhealthy emotion to any step in the thought process creates an unhealthy belief which in turn creates a life lesson.

A characteristic of the fractal design of the thought process is that it involves a sequential series of steps that has to be completed in order; I refer to this design characteristic as Fractal Sequence.

The following diagram provides the sequential steps of the Fractal Mindset Blueprint – a mathematical model for the human thought process. This model accommodates every possible thought of the present, past and future

As an example, to help explain each step, the thought process involved in buying a car will be used. While the focus will be on a logical explanation of each step, remember that an unhealthy emotion assigned to any aspect of the process will result in an unhealthy belief and attract a life lesson.

The Fractal Mindset Blueprint: Fractal Sequence

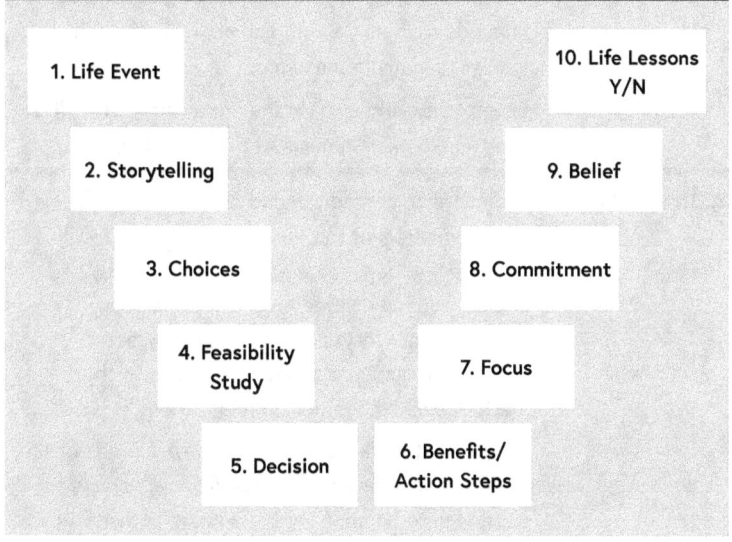

Step	Description
1. Life Event	Any stimulus that inspires you to think is considered a life event. That stimulus may relate to a thought, person, object, event, feeling, mental picture, symbol, pattern, social media post ... anything within the realms of the Universe!
	A life event can be an external stimulus such as observing a falling house brick, or an internal stimulus such as the pain felt when a house brick falls on your toe. Life events can also be a conscious stimulus such as your heart pounding out of your chest after a scare, or a subconscious stimulus such as your normal heartbeat of which you will usually be unaware.
	Example: Buying a car is the life event that we'll use to help explain each step of the blueprint.
2. Storytelling	If there is no immediate and obvious answer to the stimulus of the life event, your mind will immediately begin to tell stories to logically and emotionally understand what has been experienced. Storytelling begins the quest to assign logical and emotional values to the mathematical model which is the thought process.
	Neurologists talk about how extensive areas of the brain are stimulated by storytelling as opposed to the limited number of brain areas activated by a recital of facts. This is why sales people "don't sell the steak, they sell the sizzle", which means a potential customer will embrace the sales process more favourably if they are more neurologically engaged with the story of how the product will emotionally benefit them.

Anthropologists talk about the significance of storytelling in transferring the history and folklore of ancient civilisations from generation to generation without the benefit of written records. In short, your mind is hard-wired for storytelling.

Example: Your research on all the different cars comprise the storytelling step in buying a car. For each car, you will be telling yourself stories about visual appeal, fuel consumption, body size, price, resale value, connectivity to Bluetooth and Wi-Fi, etc., etc.

In short, does the car have "all the candy" that you are looking for? If not, then it is eliminated from your thinking. If it meets or exceeds expectation, then it is worth further consideration.

3. Choices	This step occurs only if there is no story that immediately provides an obvious explanation of the life event and represents the short list of stories that you wish to move forward with in the decision-making process, based on your wants and needs.

In this step, you are telling stories about your initial stories to develop a shortlist of possible candidate stories to further the selection process. The sooner that you discard stories that are logically inaccurate or emotionally unhealthy, then the more effective the thought process will be. Stories that you wish could be true but never will be, need to be eliminated quickly. The aim is to always be realistic and see the life event for what it truly is.

Example: Based on your wants and needs, if there is no obvious winner in your quest to buy a car, then you continue to refine your stories about each car's merits to develop a shortlist. Only very serious contenders for the title of your new car progress to step 4.

4. Feasibility Study	When an optimal story from your available choices isn't obvious, then you compare and contrast each candidate story to prioritise the best option for you based on your wants and needs. Included in this step is an analysis of each story's potential for success.
	The story that provides optimal benefits and achievable action steps is the optimal choice. The aim of any thought process and decision-making exercise is to guide you to a decision that is the best choice for you.
	Example: From your shortlist of choices in step 3 you now compare and contrast the pros and cons of each car; the aim being to identify the car that is the best option for you. If there is no clear winner, then the feasibility study continues.
5. Decision	You will notice that steps 2, 3 and 4 are a tightening spiral of storytelling. From all the potential stories to explain the life event, we cull those stories down to a list of candidate choices. If an optimal choice isn't obvious, a feasibility study is required to identify the story that provides the most beneficial, actionable option.
	The decision green lights the action steps established in the feasibility study with the benefits of the optimal story being the motivation to proceed further. The decision is the empowering step which converts preparation into execution. The decision itself is meaningless unless it is manifested into reality.

	Example: With the research and storytelling phases of buying a car now complete, the car that best suits your wants and needs is selected.
6. Benefits/ Action Steps	We do not do things unless we benefit from them – it isn't intelligent! It is the benefits of the optimal choice as established by the feasibility study that serves as the potential motivation to progress the decision to completion. To convert a decision into reality, understanding the benefits is not enough – you need executable action steps. Having potential motivation and executable action steps inspires the mental energy to manifest the decision into a reality. Example: The benefits of buying the selected car have been specified in the feasibility study. So too have the action steps to buy the car – these will include which car wholesaler/retailer to approach, who to insure with and where to obtain finance if necessary.
7. Focus	Focus is a state of mind. It is the ability to direct mental energy to a specific endeavor and reflects the priority that you give something. Understanding the benefits of your decision inspires you to focus on achievable action steps. You focus on the action steps to manifest your decision into reality. You literally become what you focus your attention on. Focus creates habit and neurological change. Example: The benefits of owning the new car provides the motivation to focus on executing the action steps. The purpose of the decision is to manifest the new car into your possession – this requires focus.

8. Commitment

Commitment can be defined as focus over time. It is a prolonged state of mind or being. You focus over time on the benefits and action steps of a decision, to the exclusion of distractions and competing priorities. A failure to commit may mean that there is a belief that creates a competing priority – and therefore a distraction.

Example: Maintaining the motivation over time to approach the wholesaler/retailer, insure and finance the car, etc., requires commitment. Losing focus with other distractions will not put the new car in your garage.

9. Belief

The purpose of every thought is to establish belief. A belief is what you believe to be true both logically and emotionally. Another word for belief is faith.

Belief is the currency of your mind in the same way that money is the currency of the economy. A healthy belief validates something that is healthy and/or invalidates something that is unhealthy. An unhealthy belief invalidates something that is healthy and/or validates something that is unhealthy.

Logically inaccurate and emotionally unhealthy values assigned to any step of the thought process creates an unhealthy belief. Healthy beliefs are realistic and well-founded. Unhealthy beliefs are unrealistic and poorly-founded.

Example: The life event was to buy a new car. If this experience is achieved then the goal of the life event may have been achieved – but was it achieved in the most emotionally healthy way?

Remember, the purpose of thought is to create and automate logically accurate and emotionally healthy beliefs. Associating an unhealthy emotion at any step of the thought process results in an unhealthy belief.

Example: Resentment towards sales staff for perceived disrespect, feeling guilty about spending money on yourself or prolonged procrastination in the decision process may result in achieving the goal of buying a new car but establish an unhealthy belief and life lesson relating to the life event.

10. Life Lesson Y/N	If the thought process is completed without any logical errors or unhealthy emotionality then the life lesson relating to the life event has been learned. Logical errors or unhealthy emotionality associated with a thought process means that the life lesson has not been learned and will recur until such time as it is learned.
	Behind every life lesson there is a noble healthy belief that has been compromised by the shock of a life event.
	The noble healthy beliefs are that you deserve to be respected by sales staff, it is ok to spend money on yourself judiciously and that you somehow benefit from procrastination. If compromised, these beliefs need to be investigated further using your preferred stress-reduction/mindfulness technique.
	The over-riding approach to a life lesson must be to change what you can, accept what you can't, but to never devalue any aspect of the experience; in the knowledge that you may never receive an explanation, apology or compensation for the inconvenience and perceived harm endured.

29: The Thought Process Is a Talent Contest

A more elaborate analogy to explain the human thought process can be drawn from the abundance of TV talent competitions which turn non-professionals into stars with recording contracts.

The aim of a TV talent show is to convert someone with sufficient style and substance into a star performing artist. Style and substance in a thought process means accurate logic and healthy emotions. The human thought process is effectively a talent show, looking to crown as the winner the most logically accurate and emotionally healthy belief that explains a life event.

The production process of a TV talent show begins with auditions being held. Judges, including the voting audience, tell themselves stories about the merits of each contestant. A recurring elimination process occurs based on what judges believe represents "talent". Semi-finals and finals are held to compare and contrast the talent/teachability/marketability of the finalists. The winner is decided. Their identified talents are nurtured over time, in a structured manner, until their market worth is hopefully realised.

If their identified talent doesn't manifest as commercial success and financial return, then a post-mortem is held and deficiencies in the franchise system are identified and learned for the next show... rinse and repeat!

The below table demonstrates the Fractal Sequence of the TV talent show.

Step	Description
1. Life Event	The life event of the TV talent show begins with the audition phase.
2. Storytelling	The auditions of the TV talent show inspire the storytelling process of the judges and home audience. These stories will be centered around the talent and appeal of each contestant. The purpose of the auditions is to provide a baseline read on which contestants have the potential to progress further.
3. Choices	Most contestants are eliminated at the first auditions of a TV talent show. Those who progress to the finals series have made it through the initial storytelling of the thought process and are shortlisted for further examination.
4. Feasibility Study	The feasibility study of the TV talent show equates to the finals series where judges compare and contrast the merits of each contestant to establish who has the most star-like qualities.

5. Decision	Proclaiming the winner of the TV talent show represents the decision step of the thought process. It is the pivotal point where the preparatory work to identify the best candidate is completed and the focus now turns to executing a mentoring program to convert the winner into a star with a recording contract and commercial success.
6. Benefits/ Action Steps	In the example of the TV talent show, the benefits are the strengths of the winning candidate. The action steps are the pre-determined mentoring program that the winner will now embark on to nurture their talent to the next level. The aptitude of the winning candidate to successfully complete the mentoring program will have been assessed in step 4, feasibility study.
7. Focus	Once the winner of the TV talent show has been selected, the focus shifts to developing the talent of the winner via a mentoring program. But having talent and a mentoring program is of no use if the winning contestant or their mentors don't exert the mental energy or focus on the tasks at hand to ensure that success is achieved.
8. Commitment	If the winner of the TV talent show handles their new-found fame poorly, then they may sabotage their opportunity for success with the competing priority of partying when they should be developing their talent. Sure, they may focus on their mentoring program spasmodically, but this doesn't represent the commitment required to create the habits and neurological change necessary to transform them into a star performer.

9. Belief	If the faith that the judges of the TV talent show placed in the winning contestant is well-founded, then the raw talent demonstrated from the audition stage will be converted to commercial success through the winner's commitment to the action steps of the mentoring program.
10. Life Lesson Y/N	If the commercial success isn't realised as expected then a review will be held of the show's casting, auditioning, judging, mentoring and commercialisation practices to establish any lessons to be learned that may improve the franchises operation of the show. Learning the life lesson for the TV show would involve implementing any identified changes to rectify any weaknesses in the way that the franchise operates.

Fractal Sequence provides the basic structure of the thought process; not unlike if you were building a suspension bridge, you would throw a line from one side of a river to the other. But a suspension bridge also has ropes that create a mesh of infrastructure to guarantee the strength, integrity and stability of the bridge itself.

The thought process also creates an internal dynamic of counter checks and balances by literally folding on itself at step 5, decision. This is where the incredible fractal design of the thought process starts to become evident – in what I refer to as Fractal Symmetry.

Part 5
Unexpected Twists and Turns

The Genius of Fractal Design

30: Fractal Symmetry

By slightly rearranging the visual presentation of Fractal Sequence it becomes obvious that the Fractal Mindset Blueprint and therefore the human thought process demonstrates a symmetrical quality. I refer to this characteristic of fractal design as Fractal Symmetry.

Each step of the blueprint inspires the next step, with the thought process pivoting on step 5, decision. Steps 2, 3 and 4 are the upwards spiral of storytelling which explains the life event and prepares you for the decision. Steps 6, 7 and 8 provide the motivation and discipline to execute on the decision and manifest it into the reality of a belief.

Stress-reduction and mindfulness techniques can be used to establish whether an emotional block is involved in preparing for a decision or in the execution of it. For example, having too many stories as choices can prevent a progression beyond steps 2, 3 and 4. Unhealthy beliefs around discipline can sabotage step 7, focus, and step 8, commitment.

Fractal Symmetry

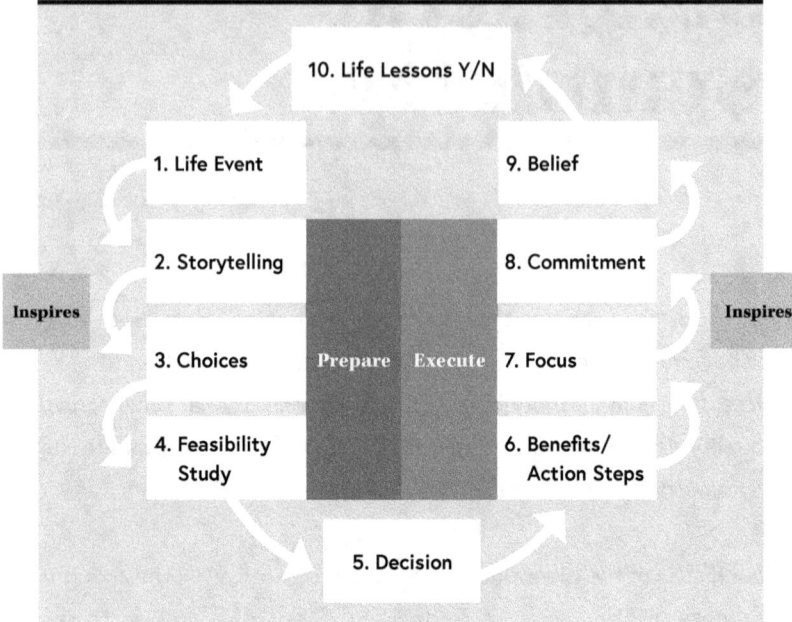

A feature of an intelligently designed computer system is that it will analyse all additions to its database and produce an error log or exception report when there is a risk to the integrity of the system. Errors and potential problems need to be investigated, resolved and signed off on by systems administrators to establish accountability.

A life lesson is the error log and exception report detailing aberrant emotional, logical, physical and energy values created by the fractal algorithm for the human thought process that runs the supercomputer which is you. The power of free will to decide whether to hold yourself accountable for their resolution is yours alone.

This is why there is an arrow in the previous illustration indicating that a life lesson creates a new life event. Unresolved emotionality creates intrusive, recurring thoughts until processed in a logically accurate and emotionally healthy way.

31: Fractal Pairing

The design characteristic of Fractal Symmetry reveals an internal dynamic of cross-checks where opposite steps of the blueprint interact to further strengthen the integrity of the thought process – not unlike the internal framework of a suspension bridge, a carpenter's ladder … or the double helix of a DNA strand! I refer to this characteristic of fractal design as Fractal Pairing.

Fractal Pairing

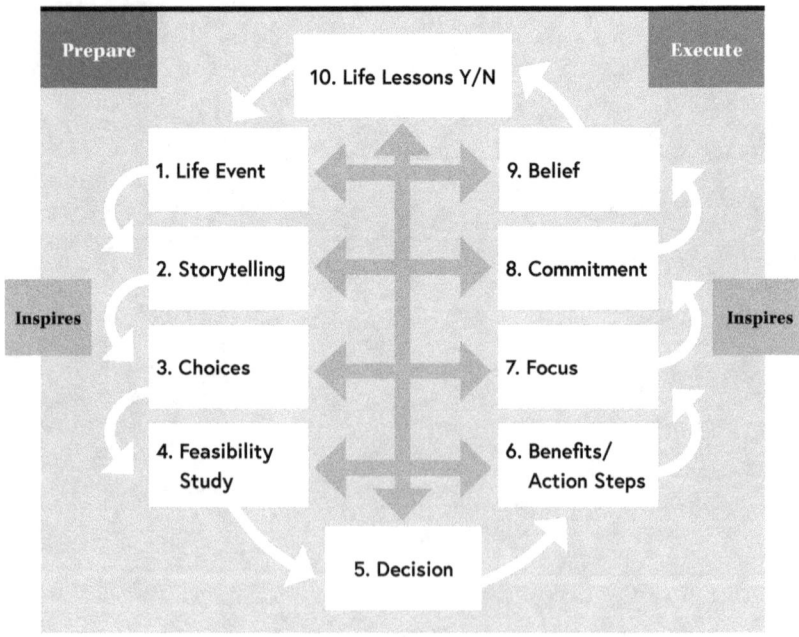

Fractal Pairing reveals a mathematical property of the fractal algorithm for the human thought process – as well as being a sequential series of steps, it is also the sum of its parts. The Fractal Mindset Blueprint has 10 steps; each of the opposing steps when added together equals 10, with the preparation and execution of step 5, decision, being treated slightly differently.

Fractal Pairing: Sum of its Parts

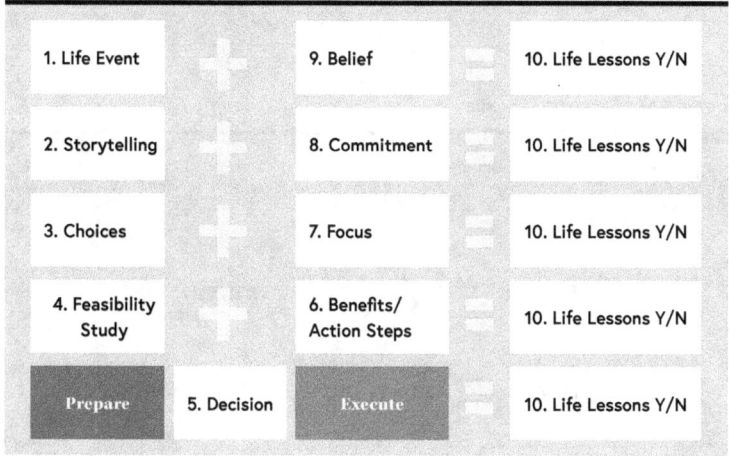

This interaction of opposite steps of the blueprint helps you to execute the preparation of the decision but also prepares you for the execution of the decision. It adds discipline and structure to the thought process in order to achieve a quality outcome.

32: Executing the Preparation of the Decision

Fractal Pairing

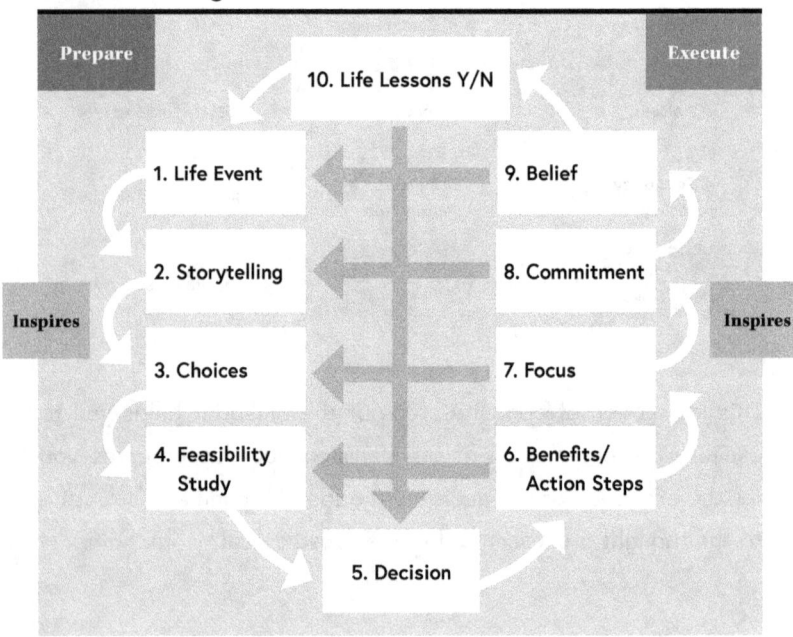

We know that beliefs are the coloured glasses which influence our interpretation of the life event. The label of "Belief" given to step 9 represents our mindset or database of beliefs as well as the belief which will be formed by the current thought process. As per the above diagram, our beliefs (step 9), relating to a life event (step 1), inspire the subsequent storytelling (step 2), to explain what the life event represents to us logically and emotionally.

To develop a complete and accurate list of all possible stories that explain the life event we must display commitment (step 8) to the storytelling (step 2) process. A commitment to the storytelling process inspires the list of viable choices (step 3).

A focus (step 7) on the individual merits of each choice culls those which don't meet our wants and needs and progresses only those which inspire closer scrutiny. In a healthy thought process, stories that are logically accurate and emotionally healthy inspire progress to the feasibility study (step 4).

A decision (step 5) on the feasibility study will be inspired by the choice which demonstrates the optimal benefits and achievable action steps (step 6). In other words, after we have compared and contrasted the pros and cons of each choice, the optimal choice from the feasibility study inspires the decision.

There is one further cross-check that promotes the integrity of the decision (step 5), and that involves the influence of "Life Lesson Y/N" (step 10). The optimal decision is always inspired by the choice with no life lessons to learn ... wherever possible.

Learning the life lesson is the ever-present self-correction mechanism which makes the thought process fractal in design. If we can self-correct and learn the life lesson live and in real-time before we finalise a decision, this is a pre-emptive strike to ensure the integrity of the thought process and ensures against making a mistake only to have to correct it later.

For example, in the finals of a TV talent show, every previously identified red flag to a contestant becoming a star performer will be scrutinised. These red flags represent life lessons for the TV show franchise and will hopefully be picked up in the selection process of steps 2 to 4. If someone can't hold a note under pressure or is considered an awkward dancer, their success will be jeopardised. The "Life Lesson Y/N" inspires a decision which avoids all red flags and the associated life lessons.

Once the decision is made, the Fractal Sequence process resumes and steps 6 to 9 involve the motivation and disciple to "lock in" the most logically accurate and emotionally healthy belief. But the second half of Fractal Symmetry also now engages to add an additional layer of integrity to the entire thought process.

33: Preparing for the Execution of the Decision

The second half of Fractal Pairing provides a quality control questioning protocol to ensure mindfulness prior to the decision so that there is clarity in its execution; not unlike how a well-nurtured child has a better chance of developing into a quality adult.

Fractal Pairing

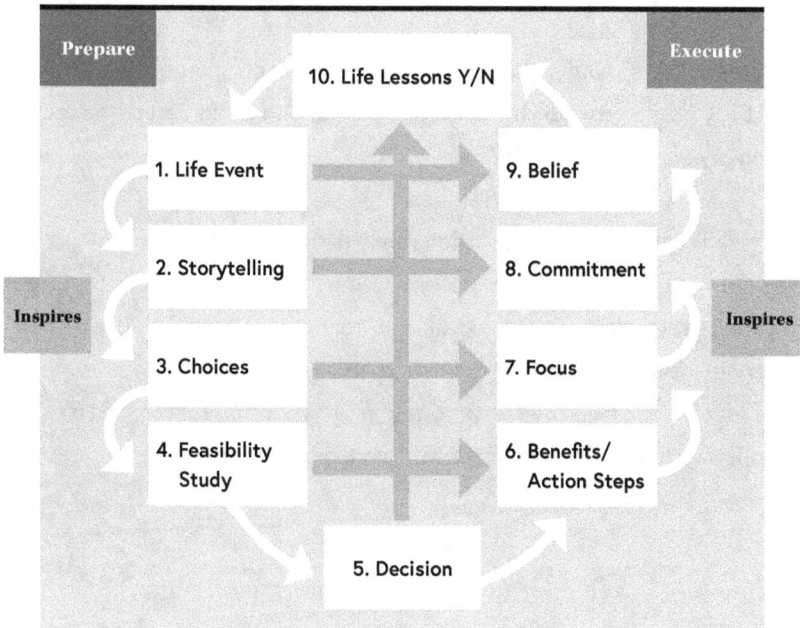

Groucho Marx, the Hollywood comedian, once said, "I refuse to join any club that would have me as a member." This quote has great relevance to our mindfulness of the stories that we tell ourselves in the thought process.

Fractal Symmetry empowers you to challenge the stories with which you genuinely want to be associated. Step 1 of the blueprint challenges you to see the life event for what it truly is, asking the questions, "Are you seeing the life event for what it realistically represents logically and emotionally?" and, "Is the tolerance range of your beliefs optimal?"

Step 2 asks the question of step 8, "Is this really a story that I want to commit to?"

Step 3 asks, "Is that story really a choice that deserves my focus?"

Step 4 asks, "Does the choice being analysed in the feasibility study really provide the optimal benefits and action steps based on my wants and needs?"

Step 5 asks, "Will this decision really attract no life lessons?"

Stress-reduction and mindfulness techniques can be used in conjunction with Fractal Sequence and Fractal Pairing to provide a detailed, structured interrogation of your thought processes relating to any topic of the past, present and future.

34: Fractal Pairing and Pattern Recognition

Pattern Formation and Pattern Recognition

Any mathematical model for intelligence and any algorithm for the human thought process must explain a major characteristic of intelligence, and that is pattern formation and pattern recognition.

Just as a chess master learns patterns of colours and the legal moves of each piece, you want to be able to immediately identify the pattern of a life event to which you have previously been exposed. Re-running a known pattern through the entire thought process is not intelligent – and nature never rewards a wasteful system!

Steps 2, 3 and 4 of the blueprint represent the tightening spiral of storytelling that whittles the candidate stories down to an optimal story. But, if at any step along the way, the optimal story becomes obvious then there must be a mechanism in the thought process to "lock in" a belief and reflexively flag the unused steps of the thought process as completed. Using Fractal Sequence, any step presupposes that previous steps of the blueprint have been attended to.

This means that there must be a shortcut to the thought process so that you can "jump the tracks" of Fractal Symmetry from the left side to the right side – cutting short the need to continue the thought process. Herein lies the beauty of Fractal Pairing.

Let's take the life event of a close friend walking towards you in the street. If it's a bright sunny day with good visibility and you immediately recognise them, then there is what I refer to as immediate "bounce back" between steps 1 and 9. You have a belief as to what the friend looks like which is immediately confirmed on seeing them, so that immediate pattern recognition negates the need for any further storytelling.

If the friend is wearing a hat then you may have to tell stories about other physical characteristics such as height, weight, or gait. If a positive identification can be made with minimal story-telling then there is "bounce back" between steps 2 and 8. You committed to the storytelling process long enough for a delayed pattern recognition.

If the friend is wearing a hat and the visibility is poor, then the "bounce back" of pattern recognition between steps 3 and 7 may take more time and require more focus.

If your friend is also the husband of your wife's sister, and he is wearing a hat in poor visibility with a woman other than your sister-in-law on his arm, when he is supposed to be away on a business trip, then the "bounce back" between steps 4 and 6 will be delayed until an exhaustive feasibility study can be performed with absolute certainty of pattern recognition.

Depending on the outcome of the feasibility study, your noble healthy beliefs will inspire a decision with no life lessons ... hopefully ... and somewhat optimistically!

This example raises two issues. Firstly, the reality is that certain life events will always have associated life lessons. Even when you win you can lose. This is why it is so important to identify and understand your noble healthy beliefs – who you wish to be and what you want to stand for in life. There is an expression that "the spirit has to be true to itself", and I believe that to be 100% accurate.

Secondly it raises a feature of the thought process and fractal design that I refer to as ... Fractal Branching.

35: Fractal Branching

Fractal Branching is a feature of fractal design whereby any of the 10 steps of the blueprint can become the first step of one or more entirely new thought processes. This explains why thought is a never-ending process in a living being. It also explains the difficulty of visualising the thought process without the assistance of enhanced computer modelling.

Your mind is a never-ending branching tree-like structure, where the trunk and each branch, twig, leaf, root and cell can communicate in a healthy or unhealthy way.

For example, in the case of the philandering brother-in-law, confirmation of suspicious circumstances will result in an explosion of branching thoughts in the form of questions – Should my wife be told? Should his wife be told? Who is the other woman? How long has this been going on? Has he done this before with other women? How many "business trips" does he go on a year? Do they have an open marriage? Should I mind my own business? Should I indulge in being blindsided by awe and pretend this chance encounter never happened?

Whilst acknowledging the complexity of Fractal Branching, my suggestion is to avoid going down the rabbit hole of exploration on this topic without the assistance of advanced computer modelling. Every thought process irrespective of complexity and intricacy calculates emotional, logical, physical and energy values which are assigned to a life event.

Fractal Branching raises a further feature of fractal design though, and one that I believe is incredibly important when using stress-reduction, mindfulness and healing techniques – Fractal Layering.

Fractal Layering

Mathematically, scattered thinking means that you are not identifying, precisely and exactly, which life event is the subject of your focus. You have an unlimited choice of life events to choose from – pick one and follow it to the logical conclusion of identifying if there is a life lesson to learn, then move to another. Remember, not making a decision is a decision in itself.

Your mind has an ability to direct its attention to any conceivable topic of the present, past and future. The object of your attention at any given time becomes the current life event in the thought process of your mind.

The life event (step 1) of observing the philandering brother-in-law inspired a storytelling process (step 2) that involved an explosion of questions. Focusing on one of those questions establishes it as the life event now under consideration – you have dropped down a fractal layer in the Fractal Branching of the thought process.

If you have ever asked a question of someone who is in emotional overload, their reply can be extremely unstructured, long winded and, to the observer, cover a long list of seemingly unrelated topics relating to the past, present and future. After an extended period, they can stop talking, give a confused look and ask what the original question was.

This doesn't mean that they are not nice people. It means that their neurophysiology is in a state of overwhelm as are their thought processes. They are skipping from layer to layer of one or more thought processes in an unhealthy, unstructured way.

Mathematically, this is crucial to understanding the social crisis of unhealthy unstructured thinking that jackpots into the mental health crisis. We are not trained to analyse one life event to its completion. We are also not taught to always focus on the noble healthy belief that has been compromised by the life event.

A good question to ask during all self-development work is, "What is the actual life event that I am focusing on and trying to unravel?"

36: Fractal Trilogy

Visually re-arranging the Fractal Sequence of the Fractal Mindset Blueprint reveals a further characteristic of fractal design. Fractal Trilogy means that there are three stages of the thought process where our mental state progresses from thinking, to doing, to being.

I first heard this phrase at a retreat offered by Dr Joe Dispenza, whose work I highly recommend. I was aware that the Fractal Mindset Blueprint could be grouped in lots of threes but could not arrive at an adequate explanation for teaching purposes.

Fractal Trilogy

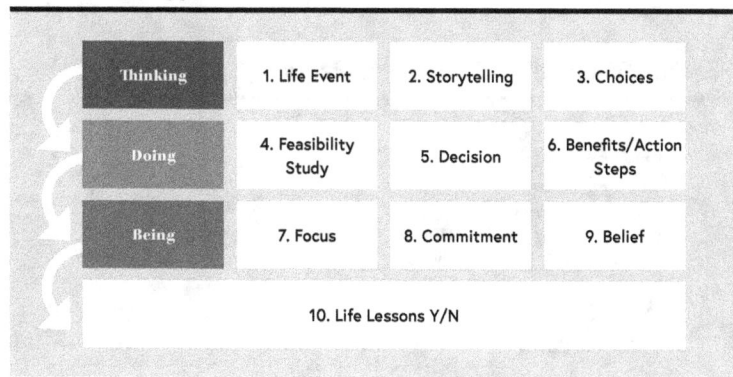

I have also heard Dr Joe refer to the thought process as a progression from thinking, to feeling, to being. As the blueprint assigns values for the optimal emotion at step 5, decision, either expression is mathematically accurate.

The thought process assigns logical and emotional values which inspires physical and energetic changes to our body and a change of consciousness to our mind/spirit. The phrase "thinking, to feeling, to being" is as equally appropriate.

Fractal Trilogy can be used with stress-reduction and mindfulness techniques to facilitate emotional congruence with each phase of Fractal Trilogy, with the progression from one phase to the next and with the sequential progression through all three phases. The aim is the emotional congruence of "you the supercomputer" at all three phases of the thought process.

The Fractal Perception Blueprint can then be illustrated mathematically as the product of its parts – meaning that 3 multiplied by 3 equals 9.

Fractal Trilogy: Product of its Parts

Thinking	1. Life Event	2. Storytelling	3. Choices
Doing	4. Feasibility Study	5. Decision	6. Benefits/ Action Steps
Being	7. Focus	8. Commitment	9. Belief
	10. If No Life Lessons then 10 = 9		

$3 + 3 + 3 = 9$

When the thought process, which is a wave of logic and emotion, is completed to create logically accurate and emotionally healthy beliefs, there are no life lessons to learn. Mathematically, in terms of the algorithm this means that for a healthy thought process steps 9 and 10 are synonymous or equal.

37: Fractal Reduction

Just as the thought process creates perception, a fractal algorithm for the human thought process, irrespective of what format it is illustrated in, must reduce and condense to a fractal algorithm for perception.

The Fractal Sequence of the Fractal Mindset Blueprint creates the Fractal Perception Blueprint. Step 2 to step 8 are the equation within the algorithm that calculates the emotional, logical, physical and energy values.

Fractal Sequence to Fractal Perception

1. Life Event	1. Life Event	1. Life Event
2. Storytelling	2. Storytelling	Logical Values
3. Choices	3. Choices	+
4. Feasibility Study	4. Feasibility Study	Emotional Values
5. Decision	5. Decision	+
6. Benefits / Action Steps	6. Benefits / Action Steps	Physical Values
7. Focus	7. Focus	+
8. Commitment	8. Commitment	Energy Values
9. Belief	9. Belief	9. Belief
10. Life Lessons Y/N	10. Life Lessons Y/N	10. Life Lessons Y/N

This ability for the longer algorithm to condense to the smaller algorithm is a feature of fractal design that I refer to as Fractal Reduction.

Fractal Symmetry to Fractal Perception

The illustration below demonstrates how Fractal Reduction applies to Fractal Symmetry as well as Fractal Sequence.

Fractal Symmetry to Fractal Perception

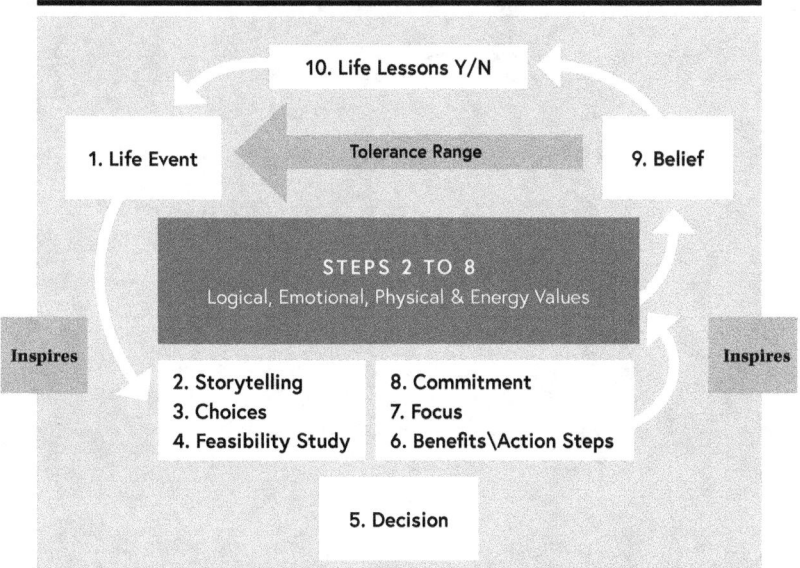

Again, our beliefs (step 9) inspire the interpretation of a life event (step 1), resulting in a thought process which assigns emotional, logical, physical and energy values (step 2 to step 8). Life lessons (step 10) accrue to any belief which is not logically accurate or emotionally healthy.

Part 6
The Encore and a Hint of Sequels!

Fractal Design –
The Shape of Things to Come

38: The Future of All Training

I was very fortunate, not long after graduating as a chiropractor at 42 years old, to be accepted into a practice management/personal development program run by Dr Scott Walker, the founder of Neuro Emotional Technique (NET) and Dr Kirby Landis, another prominent American chiropractor.

It was because of this life changing experience that I was left in no doubt that the future of all training and personal development work is for the student to be not only competent in what they are being taught, but to also be emotionally congruent with the subject matter. Let's demonstrate with two fictitious examples.

Example 1:

> A male worker on a mine site who is a really good guy; fits in well socially with co-workers, has a good sense of humour and is a potential foreman. Early on as a school kid though, he realised that he was smarter than what his grades indicated. He couldn't understand why, and ever since has reflexively devalued himself when he compared himself to others.

One quality he possessed then – and still does – was a total lack of fear and he gained the approval from school friends when he did dangerous tricks on his skateboard, BMX bike, surfboard, etc. Self-validation, risky behaviour and the approval of others then became the interconnected building blocks of a pattern.

Then he grows up to work in the safety-conscious environment of the mining industry where camaraderie is important to him but his underlying belief is that he can only receive the validation of himself and others if he is engaging in risky behaviour.

This is a demonstration of someone who is not emotionally congruent with his workplace, but if he could break that misdirected pattern, his employer would have a potentially popular foreman with an eye for identifying risky work environments and practices – because he had previously always sought them out!

Example 2:

A talented junior footballer now in his debut professional senior season; talented in attack and defence, but in see-sawing matches tends to be missing in action. Also in these games, he demonstrates inappropriate aggression towards opposition players and team-mates alike.

At the age of 10, his parents divorced acrimoniously and he would spend alternate weeks with each parent – disrupting his school and social routines. On these week-long visits, *he was also powerless to stop each parents' inquisitions about the other. After months of demonstrating anger to his parents, he was eventually allowed to live with one parent full-time.*

Changing from attack to defence and vice versa in football is referred to as transitioning – similar to repeatedly transitioning between parents as a kid. The reflexive patterning of the child which manifests in the man is that "transitioning" involves conflict, the rigours of close scrutiny and being powerless to control your environment. The only way to stop being powerless and scrutinised in a time of transition is to become angry – which stops the transitioning.

But if the belief is that anger stops transition and it's not working then he is not getting angry enough – and then the pattern escalates to team-mates.

The Fractal Mindset Blueprint and the Fractal Perception Blueprint are the underlying rules or code to every self-help and personal development program. But as demonstrated, there is no point learning something if you aren't emotionally ok with implementing it.

This book outlines the theory of a fractal algorithm for human thought. The online courses offered by Thought Martial Arts have a heavy emphasis on using the stress-reduction techniques of your choice to assist you in being emotionally congruent with thinking in a structured, emotionally healthy manner.

39: Standardised Communication

The reason why "true" artificial intelligence attracts such a heavy focus in the IT world is because it allows for a standardised protocol to enable every computer in the world to communicate together on one secure platform – the Internet of Things.

Human thinking precedes human communication; if the thought process is a precise series of steps that everyone knows, then we now have the ability to standardise communication at an individual, family, work place and societal level.

This means that by learning the patterns of a fractal algorithm for human thought you can enhance communication by understanding which step of the thought process others are on. You can also calibrate your thinking to be on the same page as them. This is very similar to if you were playing hopscotch beside someone in a playground and mimicing their steps.

For example, using the Fractal Perception Blueprint, if you are communicating with someone who is on step 4, feasibility study, and you have already made a decision and progressed to step 6, benefits/action steps, then you either have to nurture them forward or retrace and join them on step 4 or step 5.

This particularly has major ramifications for values-driven large corporations and organisations. Standardised communication means that every belief (step 9) and value (steps 2 to 8) for every policy, procedure and thought process of every employee trained within that organisation can be explained in terms of the Fractal Mindset Blueprint.

As importantly, when a policy, procedure or personnel issue arises that needs to be corrected, such a corporation/organisation can better articulate the life lesson (step 10) by explaining which step(s) of the blueprint was not executed effectively.

This logic applies equally to how we need to educate our children in standardised communication. Imagine a future generation of children who can communicate with empathy in a structured, healthy, synchronised manner!

40: Training in Collective Consciousness

For decades, the discovery of "true" artificial intelligence has been billed as potentially mankind's greatest achievement. Whether it will be implemented in an ethical way that will benefit all humanity or used as a tool of economic and societal oppression – or worse – has always been the unknown outcome.

But within an algorithm for intelligence, shouldn't there exist guidelines as to how humans can conduct themselves intelligently? ... Correct!!

Shared emotions and shared beliefs create a consciousness. The purpose of human thought is to create optimal emotional, logical, physical and energy values that serve the individual but also the collective good.

Teaching our children how to think in a healthy, structured, collective manner not only benefits their personal emotional health and resilience, it trains them in a Competency Model of Thinking which will empower them to identify or "read" patterns of unhealthy unstructured thinking in themselves and others.

The use of stress-reduction and mindfulness techniques can then help break unhealthy emotionality, broaden the tolerance range of their beliefs and reinforce noble healthy beliefs.

This ability of individuals to identify unhealthy belief patterns will also extend to the way that they view government, cultural, social, financial, corporate and economic institutions, organisations and practices. The focus will be on personal abundance, emotional, physical and spiritual health, justice and the pursuit of a meaningful and healthy existence.

Ensuring that no science or technology that can benefit humanity is withheld from the public will also be a feature of a society with a healthy collective consciousness – Nikola Tesla would have strongly approved!

41: Fractal Pairing and DNA

As illustrated on page 116, Fractal Pairing provides a structure that closely resembles the double helix of DNA. At the end of each strand of DNA are something called telomeres. I've always visualised telomeres as a structure similar in shape to a cigarette butt. Telomeres decrease in length every time that the cell reproduces.

The shortening of telomeres is a sign of aging, and ends with cell death when the integrity of the telomere is lost. Telomeres are intimately involved in the longevity of the cell.

At each end of the Fractal Mindset Blueprint, when displaying Fractal Symmetry, is step 5, decision, and step 10, "Life Lesson Y/N". The longevity of your life is based on the decisions that you make and your willingness to learn life's lessons.

This means that the longevity of your cells and the longevity of your life are both determined, or at least strongly influenced, by "structures" at the end of separate models that have the shape of a double helix – one model for DNA, the other model for human thought.

Is this just a good story derived from coincidence, or an observation of fractal design worth greater scientific investigation?

My belief is that the qualities of fractal design highlighted in this book – namely Fractal Sequence, Symmetry, Pairing, Branching, Layering, Reduction, Trilogy and Plasticity – should be of profound interest to anyone studying the intelligent design of nature. This includes brain waves, heart waves, harmonic resonance and any other phenomena suspected of having fractal properties.

Part 7
The Star Revealed

The Curtain Falls

42: The Logic of the Master Algorithm

There are many reasons why I believe that the logic of the master algorithm of artificial general intelligence (AGI) was discovered by a now deceased Australian software developer in 1999, without whom this book would never have been written.

1. The most lucrative application of AGI is to establish the Internet of Things and then clip the ticket on every transaction of global e-commerce. The software created by the deceased software developer performed, in a controlled environment, to these specifications when operational. I used the system personally.

2. This software was reviewed by a PhD-qualified consulting academic who could not disprove that the system demonstrated scalable AGI.

3. The logic of the algorithm as shown to me was a mathematical model for "enlightenment" – as it should be. There is no wave of logic and emotion in computing; it is all logic.

A unifying theory of human health and computing now means that an opinion on how the human mind works is incidental unless it is consistent with a fractal algorithm for the human thought process which:

1. Is a sequential series of steps with an ever-present self-correction mechanism which produces a perfect result in a minimum number of steps.

2. Possesses the mathematical qualities of being a series of steps which is the sum of its parts and the product of its parts.

3. Accommodates the fundamental characteristics of intelligence; namely pattern formation and pattern recognition.

4. Demonstrates qualities of fractal design namely Fractal Sequence, Symmetry, Pairing, Branching, Layering, Reduction, Trilogy and Plasticity.

5. Demonstrates how the thought process creates a fractal algorithm for perception which:
   - identifies the building blocks of emotional patterns, relating to the past, present and future.
   - explains the triggering mechanism of a belief.
   - converges physical and energetic medicine with the purpose of human thought which is to create and automate logically accurate and emotionally healthy beliefs.

43: An Australian Software Developer

As yet, I've not disclosed the name of the Australian software developer from whose work I derived the Fractal Mindset Blueprint, which dovetails into the Fractal Perception Blueprint. I have not done this as I wanted the genius of his work to be the focus. The Nobel Prize is not given posthumously, which is a great shame as I believe that he deserved it.

I was given permission by this gentleman, years before his sudden death, to write a book on his work in whatever way I saw fit, based on information that he provided – and the many questions asked and clarifications sought by me. He was buoyed by the prospect that his work could be used to help the social and medical crises caused by unhealthy mindsets.

At no stage has there ever been a non-disclosure or confidentiality agreement between us, nor was I ever asked to sign one. I have no idea how to express the Fractal Mindset Blueprint in computer code and have never pursued that endeavour.

His name was Alan Miles Metcalfe.

Acknowledgements

It's not possible to be a serial career-changer and predominant bachelor without many people to thank for their support over many years. Without the contribution of these people, this book would not have been possible.

To Dr Chris & Jane Barham – my chiropractic career and the careers of numerous others would not have been possible without your kindness and generosity of spirit.

To Dr Andrew Macfarlane – for the guidance and insight that nurtured my fascination with the mind/body complex and for sharing parallel roads less travelled.

To Ivan & Mary Walls plus the Cool Siblings – for their unwavering friendship, bed when needed and countless Sunday roasts.

To Rod McCagh – for the mateship and camaraderie of a sheep farmer with whom I've shared many a dry gully; so unnecessarily.

To Dr Peter Grant, Jennifer Morgan and of course Peter Lexo Ristovski – thank you for your friendship and honest assessment during the draft editing of this book.

To Dr David Tuffley – there is always truth in intelligent design and vice versa. Your encouragement to write this book is a fitting sequel to the genius we've witnessed. I greatly value your counsel.

To parents Charles Patrick (Mick) and Beatrice (Amy) (dec'd); siblings, Mick (Fat Chap), Mark (Wayward) and Bernadette (Lugzzz) – and to the tolerance of their partners Penny, Pat and Jon Latdog. Thank you for your support and being part of the family dynamic.

Finally, to all my patients since 2001 – as a practitioner you can't help everyone all the time but I've certainly tried to learn from each one of you. In return, hopefully you knew where to come for an honest opinion.

To paraphrase Benjamin Franklin, "The intelligent design of nature heals ... the practitioner accepts the fee."

Thought Martial Arts Online Courses

The purpose of the Thought Martial Arts online courses is to show self-aware and well-intentioned people strategies and protocols to understand emotional stress and how to rethink unhealthy emotional reflexes wired into their nervous system from childhood.

Combining information from *Logically Accurate, Emotionally Healthy* with stress-reduction/mindfulness or healing techniques, creates an enhanced technology essential to anyone interested in emotional health, mindset, performance excellence, mentoring others or effective communication.

I became a healthcare professional primarily so that I could become a better-informed patient. The Thought Martial Arts online courses have been developed by me as a committed end-user of self-development work, first and foremost.

Needless to say, if you have any concerns about your mental health, your GP or mental health professional is always your first port of call.

Life is a team game and you should always consult those practitioners in the best position to help you.

Whether you are a novice to the mindfulness revolution, a seasoned veteran or a health care professional with an interest in the mind/body connection, these online courses are a must for anyone who values their emotional health and the emotional health of their loved ones.

The global mental health crisis begins with a social crisis in unhealthy, unstructured thinking. This body of work needs to be placed in the hands of self-aware, well intentioned people because they are best placed to help others.

For future generations to live in an emotionally healthy society where anxiety and depression are the exception rather than the norm, good people such as you must lead the way.

For more information, visit https://www.thoughtmartialarts.com/

About the Author

Originally an accountant and computer systems analyst, Dr Sean Eastwood retrained as a chiropractor because of a fascination with the connection between emotional stress and physical pain. He is certified in the holistic therapeutic modality Neuro Emotional Technique (NET).

Since 2013 he has been studying the work of a now-deceased software developer who claimed to have discovered the master algorithm of artificial general intelligence (AGI) based on the idea that the human thought process is a natural law like gravity.

"We lack a pro forma guide to teach our children how to think in a healthy, structured, optimal way." says Dr Eastwood. "Simultaneously we can't program computers to mimic optimal human thought to create 'true' artificial intelligence."

Dr Eastwood's research represents a unifying theory of human health and computer science.

Step by step blueprints for human thought and perception that have the inherent fractal design of nature and accomodate all forms of physical and energetic medicine.

Alan Turing, famous for shortening WWII by cracking German ciphers as depicted in the movie *The Imitation Game*, merged mathematics, computer science, psychology and philosophy to create machine learning.

Dr Eastwood's book *Logically Accurate, Emotionally Healthy* and his Thought Martial Arts online courses are an extension of Turing's work as it applies to human health.

www.ingramcontent.com/pod-product-compliance
Lightning Source LLC
Chambersburg PA
CBHW051437290426
44109CB00016B/1599